OVERVIEW

Overview

Few people achieve lasting success in life without overcoming a few obstacles first. Consider the example of Walt Disney. As a young man, Disney was fired from his job at a newspaper because his boss thought he wasn't creative enough. His first film studio failed, leaving him bankrupt. And he struggled to release many of his now-classic films. But Disney persevered through all the setbacks he encountered and went on to build a billion-dollar entertainment corporation.

The qualities of perseverance and resilience demonstrated by Walt Disney are the same qualities you can use to be successful in the workplace. Perseverance and resilience help you cope with challenges such as losing your job, not getting the promotion you feel you deserve, losing a key customer, or missing an important deadline. By being perseverant and resilient, you're more likely to overcome such setbacks, rather than panic or give up.

This course outlines strategies for dealing with workplace setbacks. These strategies can help you rebound quickly from them, refocus on your goals, and ultimately succeed. This course also describes how you can learn to be perseverant and resilient, yourself. And it provides strategies you can use to enhance and develop your levels of perseverance and resilience. Adopting these strategies should boost your ability to cope with crises when they occur.

After taking this course, you should be in a better position to manage setbacks, challenges, and adversity at work using the techniques of perseverance and resilience you have learned.

Setting a challenging goal for yourself can be an extremely rewarding experience. It forces you to grow personally, and helps you to reap benefits that you may previously have thought unlikely. But few things are as frustrating as watching your best-laid plans come apart as a result of an unforeseen obstacle. That's why you need to persevere and overcome any setbacks in order to achieve your goal.

To achieve your targets and objectives, you need to set an inspiring goal that will help you to stay motivated. Remember that no matter how determined you may be, you should also be prepared for possible setbacks along the way. And bear in mind that the ultimate test of your perseverance and resilience will be your ability to deal effectively with, and overcome, any obstacles you encounter.

In this course, you'll learn how to set inspiring goals that will give you a sense of direction by making them measurable, achievable, purposeful, and specific. You're more likely to succeed in your goal if it's energizing and

Perseverance and Resilience

well planned. You'll then discover how to anticipate setbacks by listing potential obstacles, categorizing and prioritizing them, and then identifying the key obstacle.

Finally, you'll examine how to overcome obstacles by recognizing where your plan went wrong and by reaffirming your abilities. This process also involves refocusing on your goal, and resuming with a new plan of action.

By following the guidelines in this course, you'll be better able to proactively anticipate and plan for possible difficulties. And you'll have a greater chance of overcoming obstacles and achieving your goal by using perseverance and resilience.

When was the last time you experienced a setback or failure? In all walks of life, every person will meet with disappointment at some point. An even greater failure, however, is to leave these setbacks unassessed. Those who don't accurately dissect their errors are likely to make them again.

To persevere beyond a setback, you must analyze it to find its root causes. You'll benefit from dissecting what went wrong and why it went wrong. From there you can realize the changes needed to avoid the same fate again.

A setback can linger in people's minds such that they allow it to define them. A lack of closure – wherein you fail to understand why the setback occurred – can result. This feeling blocks you from adapting to new challenges and experiences.

By analyzing your setback and viewing it as a learning opportunity, you can move beyond it.

Sorin Dumitrascu

In this course, you'll learn about perseverance and the qualities that give you the ability to bounce back. This involves a number of skills including determination, improvisation, and realism.

Turning a setback into lessons learned again requires perseverance and is a multi-layered process. This involves finding out what the setback is, why it happened, learning lessons from it, and documenting these lessons.

This course also shows you how you can embrace the lessons you've learned. There are several strategies to help this process including re-evaluating your goals and establishing a regained sense of confidence.

This course helps you develop positive lessons from changes brought about by setbacks. Once mastered, this ability to bounce back through perseverance and resilience will be a great advantage.

CHAPTER 1 - Developing Character for Perseverance and Resilience

CHAPTER 1 - Developing Character for Perseverance and Resilience

Section 1 - Dealing with Setbacks
Section 2 - Learning to Persevere
Section 3 - Boosting Your Resilience
Section 4 - Strategies of Resilience and Perseverance

Section 1 - Dealing with Setbacks
Section 1 - Dealing with Setbacks

Setbacks and challenges are an inevitable part of life – and work. It often takes several attempts to get something right. Long-term success is rarely achieved without a few setbacks along the way.

Unless you interpret a setback at work constructively, you might internalize it and take it personally. This may cause you to react to the setback in self-disparaging ways that undermine your self-confidence. It can also distract you from finding solutions.

Accepting the inevitability of setbacks

Accepting the inevitability of setbacks

It's normal to experience setbacks as you progress through life. These are the unexpected or sudden events that can derail your plans and cause you to fail or be rejected. Long-term success is rarely achieved without a few setbacks along the way.

You can bounce back from setbacks – even the most devastating ones. For example, many successful entrepreneurs witness the failure of their first business ventures. Some of these ventures are even declared bankrupt along the way. However, these people know that success is rarely achieved on the first try. So they persevere with their plans, work harder, and find other ways of achieving their goals.

Setbacks shouldn't be confused with the common challenges you face every day in the workplace, such as dealing with a heavy workload, a difficult customer, or a tight deadline. Setbacks are concerned with bigger and more substantial issues.

For example, losing your job, failing to get the promotion you expected, or receiving a very poor performance review are all considered setbacks. Making a mistake that obstructs the work of your team for weeks or that negatively affects key customers could also be considered a setback.

And taking actions that result in a huge number of products being recalled or that bring bad press to your company are even more serious setbacks.

Setbacks and challenges are an inevitable part of life – and work. Even if you try your best, you won't necessarily succeed. It often takes several attempts to get something right.

Setbacks shouldn't discourage you from trying again. In fact, you should regard setbacks as

opportunities to learn something new, to grow in character, and to change direction. With the right mind-set, you can use any setback you encounter to move you closer to achieving your ultimate goal.

Consider the example of Soichiro Honda. As a young man, his early engineering designs were rejected. People even laughed at them. However, Honda didn't give up. He kept working at his designs and went on to start his own business, the Honda Corporation. This eventually became a billion-dollar enterprise.

Question

Decide whether each workplace incident is a regular challenge or a major setback by matching the correct label to each example. Each label can be used more than once.

Options:

Perseverance and Resilience

A. A regular challenge
B. A major setback

Targets:

1. Losing your most important customer because you made a mistake
2. Working with an unfriendly person, who you don't like
3. Having to perform a difficult task that you don't enjoy
4. Revealing information that damages your company's reputation

Answer

Losing an important customer because you made a mistake is a major setback. You shouldn't let setbacks discourage you.

Working with an unfriendly person you don't like is a regular challenge. You may face challenges like this each day.

Having to perform a task you don't enjoy is a regular challenge. Setbacks are concerned with bigger and more substantial issues.

Revealing information that damages your company's reputation is a major setback. You can bounce back from setbacks – even the most devastating ones.

Internalizing setbacks as failures

Internalizing setbacks as failures

When you encounter a setback at work, you can react in two ways. You might interpret the setback as a mere detour on the road to success. Or you might internalize it by taking the setback personally and allowing it to influence your beliefs about yourself. As a result, your self-esteem may suffer. So instead of focusing your energy on developing a plan to deal with the initial setback, you may start to experience negative emotions and to react in negative ways.

In the workplace, a setback usually provokes two kinds of negative emotions – a fear of rejection and a fear of failure. Both emotions are normal. The problem isn't failure or rejection in themselves – all that matters is how you deal with them.

You can deal with your fears in a calm, controlled way that focuses on rebounding from the negative incident.

Or, you can internalize your fears by interpreting them in a self-disparaging way – a way that undermines your own abilities.

For example, when your work is criticized by your manager, you might experience a fear of disapproval or rejection. Internalizing this fear may result in you feeling embarrassed or humiliated. You might even feel incompetent or depressed.

If you lose a large sum of money by making an unwise investment, you might experience a fear of failure. Internalizing this fear may cause you to feel powerless or despondent. Or you might react in a panicked or angry way.

Self-disparaging interpretations of the setbacks you encounter are likely to cause you to feel discouraged and defeated. Ultimately, they may cause you to feel that you're not good enough. You'll probably spend more time worrying about the setback than trying to find a solution.

Reacting in such a counterproductive manner prevents you from constructively evaluating your setbacks. Unless you can take setbacks in your stride, learn from them, and move forward, it's likely you'll shy away from life's challenges in the future. This could hold you back from reaching your goals.

Question

Take a moment to consider your own reaction to setbacks at work.

When you encounter a setback, how do you usually react?

Options:

1. Always internalize the setback
2. Sometimes internalize the setback

3. Never internalize the setback

Answer

Option 1: You say you always internalize the setbacks you encounter. You should avoid doing this, as it's likely to make you feel discouraged and defeated.

Option 2: You indicate that you sometimes internalize setbacks. You should try to minimize this behavior, so you can deal more productively with setbacks in the future.

Option 3: That's great! By never internalizing failures or rejections, you should be able to deal constructively with any setbacks you encounter.

Consider Chang's situation. He's a project manager in a software company and has just suffered a major setback. His team spent months designing a software product for a key customer. Unfortunately, the end product doesn't have all the technical capabilities the customer requested. As a result, the customer is threatening not to pay.

Follow along as Chang discusses the setback with his colleague, Maria.

Maria: What's up, Chang? You look really stressed.

Maria is concerned.

Chang: I am. I'm in big trouble – I've made a mess of the Kimball project. I'm a failure.

Chang is panicking.

Maria: What's happened?

Maria is curious.

Chang: My team developed a brilliant product that doesn't contain several key functions that my client specifically requested. I guess I misunderstood what the client was looking for. I've been told Kimball won't pay for this product, which means I've wasted a lot of our company's resources and money. I feel so humiliated.

Perseverance and Resilience

Chang is humiliated.

Maria: Maybe your client could use the existing product free of charge until you develop an upgraded version that meets all the requirements? That way, you'll retain Kimball as a customer. And it might not take too long to add in the extra functionality.

Maria is helpful.

Chang: I don't know about that. I'm pretty sure Kimball is going to take its business elsewhere from now on. I think I'm about to be sidelined too. My manager walked right by me a few minutes ago without saying anything. I feel so stupid. Maybe I'm just not up to the job.

Chang is worried.

Chang clearly made a mistake by misunderstanding his client's requirements. But instead of taking a deep breath and resolving to deal with the problem calmly and effectively, he's internalized the setback. As a result, he's feeling anxious, incompetent, and humiliated. By overreacting to the setback in this way, Chang fails to focus his energy on possible solutions.

It's how you respond to a failure that matters, not the failure itself. There's a big difference between failing at something and being labeled a failure.

The way you explain things to yourself usually determines the way you subsequently act. And the way you interpret what's going on around you largely determines your emotions. So if you interpret setbacks in a constructive way, you're more likely to remain calm, to learn from them, and to move on.

Try to keep your thoughts in perspective – a setback is unlikely to ruin your image. After all, no one gets through life without making mistakes. And people are generally more interested in their own failures and setbacks than yours.

Question

Which are examples of statements where setbacks are being internalized?

Options:

1. "After I experience a setback at work, I'm afraid I look like a failure to my colleagues."

2. "I failed to save my business, so I must be a failure myself."

3. "I didn't reach my sales target, so I'm obviously lazy and incompetent."

4. "All I can think about is how stupid I looked, so now I just want to give up."

5. "I failed to meet my deadline, so the deadline was clearly too tight."

6. "When I experience a setback, I try to learn from it and move on."

Answer

Option 1: This option is correct. A fear of rejection or failure is a normal reaction to a setback. However, problems occur when these fears are internalized.

Option 2: This option is correct. Failing to distinguish the difference between failing at something and being labeled a failure shows that the failure has been internalized.

Option 3: This option is correct. Failure is internalized by interpreting it in a self-disparaging way.

Option 4: This option is correct. When you spend more time worrying than focusing on a solution, you've internalized the setback.

Perseverance and Resilience

Option 5: This option is incorrect. When you internalize a setback, you usually interpret it in a way that undermines your own abilities.

Option 6: This option is incorrect. Internalizing a setback usually prevents you from reacting calmly, learning from it, and moving on.

Section 2 - Learning to Persevere
Section 2 - Learning to Persevere

Successful people achieve their goals by persevering through the daily challenges of life. They use perseverance to overcome whatever obstacles they encounter in the workplace.

You can take steps to develop your levels of perseverance. Try to make perseverance a habit that you practice every day. Remember to focus on your goals and to never give up. Nurture a vision and keep it in mind as you engage in your daily work activities. And find ways to develop a sense of resilience.

Defining perseverance

The most successful people in life don't just sit back and wait for success. Instead, they achieve success by persevering through the daily challenges of life. They continuously move forward, despite the obstacles that sometimes appear in front of them. Perseverant people buckle down, work hard, and keep going. They're usually optimistic, and see the positive in every situation. And they're strongly motivated to achieve their goals.

To develop perseverance, you should have a vision for what you want to achieve in life and stay focused on that vision. When things go wrong, you must remain strong. Even the biggest setbacks can be overcome with the right mentality. However, perseverance only works when you're in control of your problems and have the power to solve them. Perseverance won't necessarily solve problems that are outside your realm of control.

Perseverance can be regarded as a personality trait. To persevere, you need to have the right attitude – an attitude of persistent determination or tenacity. To display a tenacious attitude, you need to keep going whenever you're feeling tired or discouraged, and never give up. Everyone has a degree of perseverance, which can be improved over time and developed to its full potential. So everyone can learn the skill of perseverance and can benefit from a tenacious attitude.

Question

In what ways do you think you could benefit by learning to persevere?

Options:

1. You're better able to overcome setbacks at work
2. You're more likely to accomplish what you set out to do
3. You increase your chances of being successful in life
4. You're more likely to succeed the first time you try something
5. You're better able to solve problems that are outside your control

Answer

Option 1: This option is correct. By persevering, you'll be able to deal with setbacks at work more easily. This should help you to be a more successful employee.

Option 2: This option is correct. By learning to persevere, you're more likely to accomplish what you set out to do in life. You'll find it easier to rebound from setbacks and to refocus on your goals.

Option 3: This option is correct. When you persevere, you increase your chances of being successful in life. Few

Perseverance and Resilience

people achieve lasting success without persevering and overcoming a few obstacles first.

Option 4: This option is incorrect. Persevering doesn't mean you're more likely to succeed the first time you try something. Perseverant people often make numerous attempts before they eventually succeed. However, they never give up.

Option 5: This option is incorrect. Perseverant people don't focus on problems that are outside their control or that they don't have the power to solve. Perseverance only works when people are in control of their problems.

At work, perseverance can benefit you by helping you overcome setbacks and accomplish goals. By persevering, you're more likely to be successful. Perseverance requires steady effort, strong will, and staying power. It allows you to deal with setbacks and challenges that others may find too difficult.

Question

Which statements describe an attitude of perseverance?

Options:

1. Ahmed is optimistic and strongly motivated to complete his project on time

2. José has a clear vision for what he wants to achieve in the next ten years

3. Judith is constantly trying to solve problems that are outside her control

4. Carla gives up easily, but believes she can learn to be more perseverant

5. Mei is content to wait passively for success, as she believes she's destined to be successful eventually

6. Frank doesn't let obstacles prevent him from achieving his goals

Answer

Option 1: This option is correct. Perseverant people are usually optimistic, in that they see the positive in every situation. And they're strongly motivated to achieve their goals. They achieve success by persevering through daily setbacks, difficulties, and challenges.

Option 2: This option is correct. People who are perseverant have a vision for what they want to achieve in life and stay focused on that vision. When things go wrong, they don't give up – they remain strong. They keep working toward the goals they want to achieve.

Option 3: This option is incorrect. Perseverance requires you to focus your attention on what is in your control. If you can't influence something or affect a particular outcome, you should leave it aside and concentrate on what you can influence.

Option 4: This option is correct. Perseverance can be regarded as a personality trait. Everyone has a degree of perseverance, which can be improved over time and developed to its full potential. So everyone can learn the skill of perseverance.

Option 5: This option is incorrect. Perseverant people don't sit back and wait for success. Instead, they achieve success by persevering through the daily challenges of life.

Option 6: This option is correct. People who are perseverant are continuously moving forward, despite the obstacles that sometimes appear in front of them. They tend to buckle down, work hard, and keep going.

Ways of developing perseverance

While everyone has a degree of perseverance, most people don't seek to develop it to its full potential. This is a mistake, as a perseverant attitude can help you achieve your goals and be successful in life. Luckily, perseverance is a personality trait that can be cultivated with a little effort.

You can take steps to develop your levels of perseverance. First, try to make perseverance a habit that you practice every day. Next, remember to focus on your goals and to never give up. You should nurture a vision and keep it in mind as you engage in your daily work activities. And you should find ways to develop a sense of resilience.

1. Make perseverance a habit

You should try to make perseverance a habit – something you get used to doing each day without even thinking about it. When perseverance becomes second nature, you'll find you keep trying when others give up. You'll stick to a task when problems and challenges arise. And you'll keep working at it even when you don't feel like doing it and you'd prefer to give up.

By making perseverance a habit, you'll be in a better position to pursue your goals in a focused way. You'll be able to steadily work toward your objectives, even when the path to the end is strewn with difficulties.

For example, people who make perseverance a habit are more likely to see projects through to the end, to deal with problems when they arise, and to be solutions-oriented. They're usually able to focus on overall goals and objectives.

2. Focus and never give up

To develop perseverance, you need to focus on your goals and objectives in a single-minded way. If you jump from one activity to another or from idea to idea, you won't see any task through to fruition and probably won't be successful either. No matter how talented you are, your talents can never be maximized without perseverance.

There is a direct link between perseverance and potential. So if you give up easily, you'll have to overcome this personality trait to be successful. Otherwise, opportunities may be lost and you may never reach your full potential.

For example, people who are focused and who don't give up easily are likely to make successful entrepreneurs. Such people usually have the staying power and determination required to tackle the diverse challenges of starting a business.

3. Nurture a vision

Perseverance and Resilience

Perseverant people tend to create and nurture a vision of what they want to achieve. This vision is what motivates them to persevere to the end of the road, despite the difficulties and challenges they may encounter along the way.

When you nurture a vision, you display an optimistic outlook to the people around you. You tend to believe all your efforts will be rewarded with great results and success in the end. Your vision gives you the strength to toil away at a task from start to finish, no matter how arduous it seems or how long it takes.

For example, people who have a clear mental image of what they ultimately want to achieve are unlikely to be deterred by obstacles or to give up. They're more likely to see obstacles as temporary setbacks that need to be faced and dealt with, before getting back on track again.

4. Develop resilience

To persevere in life, you should develop a sense of resilience. Resilient people don't let challenges and problems defeat them. Instead, they bounce back from whatever setbacks or disappointments they encounter, no matter how badly they feel. And they continue to move toward their goals.

You can use perseverance when you're in control of your problems and have the power to solve them. But you'll need to show resilience when you're not in control of the factors that are setting you back.

For example, if you experience a major setback that's outside your control, such as losing your job, you'll need to draw on all your powers of resilience to remain positive as you search for other employment.

By developing your levels of perseverance, you'll be able to display a strong will and a sense of determination at difficult times. You'll also be able to take purposeful action in the face of adversity. And you're more likely to make the most of your talents and to be successful in meeting your goals.

Question

Sonia is a manager in a gaming company. She's just realized that the presentation she's been working on for weeks has been deleted accidentally. As a result, she's going to have to redo all of her work. But she's scheduled to deliver the presentation to a group of potential investors in a few days, so she doesn't have much time.

Sonia could simply cancel the presentation. But she prefers to stay at a task when problems arise rather than give up. So for the next three days, she focuses single-mindedly on re-creating the presentation. She knows her presentation could convince the audience to invest in the company and she's determined to do a good job.

She doesn't allow this setback to discourage her or to affect her in a negative way. She bounces back quickly from the experience and goes on to deliver an excellent presentation.

In what ways does Sonia show that she's developed an attitude of perseverance?

Options:

1. She prefers to stay with the difficult task of re-creating the presentation when others might walk away

2. She focuses single-mindedly on her objective of completing the presentation on time and doesn't give up

Perseverance and Resilience

3. She creates and nurtures a vision of how her presentation could convince the audience to invest in the company

4. She doesn't let the setback discourage her and she bounces back quickly from it

5. She realizes quickly that she will have to re-do all of her work

6. She's capable of delivering an excellent presentation to an important audience

Answer

Option 1: This option is correct. Sonia has made perseverance a habit. She stays at a task when problems and challenges arise. And she keeps toiling away when it's easier to admit defeat.

Option 2: This option is correct. Sonia focuses on her goal and doesn't give up. She realizes that if she jumps from one activity to another, she won't see any task through to fruition.

Option 3: This option is correct. Sonia has successfully nurtured a vision of what she wants to achieve. This vision is what motivates her to persevere and to complete the presentation on time, despite the challenges she encounters.

Option 4: This option is correct. Sonia has developed a sense of resilience. She doesn't let challenges and problems defeat her. Instead, she bounces back from them – no matter how badly she feels.

Option 5: This option is incorrect. When Sonia realizes she must complete the presentation again, she isn't displaying perseverance. However, she displays perseverance in the manner in which she deals with this problem.

Sorin Dumitrascu

Option 6: This option is incorrect. The ability to deliver an excellent presentation to an important audience isn't in itself an act of perseverance.

Section 3 - Boosting Your Resilience

Section 3 - Boosting Your Resilience

You can't prevent negative events from occurring in life – but you can minimize their consequences by being resilient. The way you think and behave when faced with adversity demonstrates how resilient you are.

You can improve your resilience at work in different ways. One way is to recognize and use your personal strengths in the workplace. Another way is to make an effort to build good relationships with your colleagues at work. You can also take decisive action and do whatever needs to be done to achieve your goals. And you can nurture yourself and look after your own health and well-being.

The importance of being resilient

The importance of being resilient

Perseverance is an attitude that keeps you going whenever you're feeling discouraged. To improve your perseverance, you need to develop your resilience. Resilience involves remaining calm when challenging events occur. You particularly need resilience when you're not in control of the factors setting you back and you can't solve the problem yourself. You can't avoid bad things happening in life – but you can minimize their negative consequences by being resilient.

Resilience means you can choose to be a survivor, not a victim. You're more likely to look for ways of tackling your problems than to complain about your bad luck. Resilient people are usually better at managing their workplace relationships too. By being resilient, you interact in a more positive way with the people around you, and you encourage them to be positive too.

Perseverance and Resilience

Question

Clara has just been told that she's lost her job due to downsizing. When she hears the news, she bursts into tears. She's not sure what she's going to do next and she feels scared and worthless.

However, Clara's shock subsides in a couple of hours. She quickly realizes the decision to make her redundant is not a reflection of her value as a person. She starts working on her résumé right away and enrolls with an employment agency on the way home.

Do you think Clara displays resilience?

Options:

1. Yes
2. No

Answer

Option 1: This is the correct option. Despite her initial feelings of shock and panic, Clara shows resilience by taking immediate actions to find another job, instead of simply complaining or feeling sorry for herself. She also reaffirms her own value as a person.

Option 2: This option is incorrect. Clara is initially shocked and panicked, which is a normal reaction to a major setback. But she quickly regains her composure and reminds herself of her own value. She proves she's a survivor, not a victim, by taking positive actions to find another job right away.

The qualities of perseverance and resilience are closely linked to self-motivation – the internal force that drives you forward in life. Self-motivation pushes you to achieve, produce, develop, and grow. When you feel like giving up or when you don't know how to start something, it's your self-motivation that gets you going and sustains you. You need self-motivation to reach your goals in life.

How resilient do you think you are? You may not even know for sure until you have to deal with a serious challenge. Although some people are naturally very resilient, anyone can learn to develop more resilience. While you can't always control what happens to you in life, you can control your responses. The way you react to adversity will demonstrate how resilient you are.

Question

Which statements describe an attitude of resilience?

Options:

1. Natasha interacts in a positive way with her colleagues at work and she encourages them to be positive too

2. Manuel rebounds quickly after losing his two most valuable customers

3. Amelie motivates herself to achieve her weekly goal of submitting the financial reports on time

4. Lars constantly complains about his long run of bad luck and fears that things won't improve

5. Dominique doesn't bounce back easily, and she accepts that there's nothing she can do about this

Answer

Option 1: This option is correct. Resilient people are usually better at managing their workplace relationships than non-resilient people. Life can be much more difficult for people who don't have this skill.

Option 2: This option is correct. Being a resilient person means you're able to bounce back from the setbacks and disappointments of daily life, instead of being defeated by them. Resilience means you can choose to be a survivor, not a victim.

Option 3: This option is correct. The qualities of perseverance and resilience are closely linked to self-motivation – the internal force that drives you forward in life and keeps you going. Self-motivation pushes you to achieve, produce, develop, and grow.

Option 4: This option is incorrect. Resilient people are more likely to look for ways of tackling their problems than to grumble and complain about their bad luck. They are survivors, not victims.

Option 5: This option is incorrect. Resilience is a learned behavior and nearly everyone can learn to be resilient. While you can't always control what happens to you in life, you can control your responses.

Ways of developing resilience

Ways of developing resilience

Resilience can be displayed in a variety of ways. For example, some people display their resilience by being optimistic and resourceful when faced with daunting challenges. Others do so by being determined and strong willed. Resilience can also be displayed by teams when members support each other at work and collaborate to solve problems creatively.

External factors such as poverty, ill health, and a lack of social support may have a negative impact on your well-being and ability to achieve. For example, they can lead to depression and poor performance at work.

However, many people use the challenges in their lives as springboards for growth and future success. In other words, they don't let the challenges in their lives define them or label them. They draw on their resiliency to overcome problems and go on to build satisfying, productive lives.

For example, Orville and Wilbur Wright battled depression and family illness, but these setbacks didn't hold them back – they went on to invent and build the world's first successful airplane. Oprah Winfrey was born into poverty and endured a difficult childhood. But she overcame these early misfortunes and has become one of the most popular TV icons of her time.

You may have noted that you can foster and improve your resilience at work in various ways. One way is to recognize and use your personal strengths in the workplace. Another way is to make an effort to build good relationships with your colleagues at work. You can also take decisive action whenever necessary and do whatever needs to be done to achieve your goals. And you can nurture yourself and look after your own health and well-being.

Recognize your personal strengths

To improve your resiliency, you should recognize your own personal strengths. Your strengths might include your communication skills, your creativity, your ability to work hard, or the fact you're a quick learner or a team player. Take steps to become more aware of your strengths. You can do this by asking friends or colleagues who know you well what strengths they believe you possess. When you know what your strengths are, you can decide to use them more often. In particular, you can resolve to apply them in difficult situations.

For example, if you know you're a hard worker, a quick learner, and very adaptable, you'll be able to cope with major changes in your work environment, such as a restructuring or a merger. You won't be overly daunted by working with new people or by taking on a new role.

Build good relationships

You can improve your resiliency by building good relationships with your work colleagues. For many people, this is the single most effective way of becoming more resilient. If you have a great relationship with your manager and colleagues, you'll be able to access support and encouragement when you need it. You'll also be able to share ideas about how to solve workplace problems. As a result, you'll be better able to cope with stress, pressure, and workplace challenges when they arise.

For example, if you find yourself dealing with a difficult customer and don't know how to proceed, consulting with more experienced colleagues for advice and guidance could prove to be extremely helpful.

Take action

Another way to improve your resiliency is to take decisive action when necessary. When you're resilient, you don't see challenges and crises as insurmountable problems. Nor do you detach from your problems and wish they would go away. Instead, you regard problems as obstacles that can be overcome. You're willing to step forward and take whatever actions are necessary to deal with the difficulties you find yourself in. You also keep things in perspective and avoid blowing setbacks out of proportion.

For example, if you feel you're not developing your skills by working on a particular team and would be more productive working on a different team, you won't sit back and do nothing. You're more likely to meet with your manager and offer convincing arguments as to why you should move. You'll do all in your power to improve your personal situation.

Nurture yourself

You can improve your resilience by nurturing yourself and looking after your overall well-being. You can nurture yourself by getting regular exercise, ensuring you're well rested, and that you eat a healthy diet.

You can also nurture yourself by learning how to relax and unwind when you're away from work. For example, this might involve taking a vacation – or simply a walk or short break. You should also take part in activities that you enjoy and find relaxing, and that give your brain a rest from work. Many people find practices like yoga and meditation help them to unwind.

Consider Jack's situation. Jack works as a financial analyst in a bank and he knows that in order to reach his potential, he should become more resilient. He realizes he's a very organized, methodical person. So every time he suffers a setback, he writes a list of the steps he can take to overcome the obstacle he's facing.

Jack decides to attend a conference on insurance trends, as he feels his knowledge of this area needs to be expanded. He deals with the stress of his job by taking a walk at lunch break each day with some colleagues. They support him during difficult times and provide advice when needed.

Jack wants to stay fit and healthy. He eats a balanced diet and goes to the gym twice a week. He knows that when he's tired, he doesn't perform well. So he tries to ensure he gets plenty of rest each night.

By developing his resilience, Jack will be better able to deal with the setbacks and disappointments life throws his way. This should help him to be more successful at work. And he's more likely to maintain a positive outlook and to reach his full potential.

Question

Match each method of boosting resiliency with the example that corresponds to it.

Options:

A. Recognize personal strengths
B. Build good relationships
C. Take action
D. Nurture yourself

Targets:

1. Rick knows he's an excellent communicator, so decides to go ahead and make a speech even though his notes have been mislaid

2. Mizuki's colleagues support and encourage her after the contract she's been trying to win for months is awarded to a competitor

3. Sally can't concentrate in the office, as there's too much noise, so she arranges to move to a quieter position on another floor

4. Fazal meditates twice a week and takes a short vacation at the end of a stressful period at work

Answer

Knowing that he's an excellent communicator, and opting to make a speech without notes, is an example of Rick recognizing his personal strengths. When you know what your strengths are, you can decide to use them more often.

The fact that Mizuki receives her colleagues' support and encouragement after the contract she's been trying to win is awarded to a competitor demonstrates that she has

Perseverance and Resilience

built good relationships in her workplace. If you have a great relationship with your colleagues, you'll be better able to cope with workplace challenges when they arise.

When Sally arranges to move to a quieter position on another floor, she takes decisive action to solve her problem. Resilient people are willing to step forward and take whatever actions are necessary.

By meditating twice a week and taking vacations at the end of stressful periods, Fazal demonstrates that he nurtures himself. You can also nurture yourself by getting regular exercise, ensuring you're well rested, and by eating a healthy diet.

Section 4 - Strategies of Resilience and Perseverance

Section 4 - Strategies of Resilience and Perseverance

There are three strategies you can use to develop and maximize your levels of perseverance and resilience. The first strategy is to ensure your emotions don't control your actions. To do this, you should understand – and master – the negative emotions you feel when you experience a setback. Also, avoid letting your emotions dictate your decisions.

The second strategy is to expect setbacks to occur and to accept that they're an inevitable part of life. So always expect the unexpected. Prepare yourself mentally for unforeseen events, challenges, and outcomes and develop backup plans to help you cope.

The third strategy is to regard setbacks as opportunities for growth, change, and success, rather than as problems that can't be overcome. To do this, you should change your perspective on setbacks, so you don't interpret them in a defeatist way.

Learning to control emotions

Learning to control emotions
There's a strong link between perseverance and resilience. If you're a perseverant person – who keeps going when you encounter difficulties and finishes every task that you start – you're likely to have a resilient character too. There are strategies you can use to maximize your levels of perseverance and resilience. You can use these strategies to help you cope with the inevitable setbacks that occur in the workplace. They'll also help you to stay focused on your overall goals.

You can use three strategies to develop and maximize your levels of perseverance and resilience. The first strategy is to ensure your emotions don't control your actions. The second strategy is to expect setbacks to occur and to accept that they're an inevitable part of life. And the third strategy is to regard setbacks as opportunities for growth, change, and success, rather than as problems that can't be overcome.

The first strategy you can use is to ensure your emotions don't control your actions. To do this, try to understand – and master – the negative emotions you feel when you fail at something or are rejected by somebody. These emotions may include feelings such as embarrassment, humiliation, depression, panic, and anger. Often, the reason you fail has little to do with you and more to do with other people or external forces. So your emotional reaction may be exaggerated or irrational.

Having an irrational or exaggerated emotional response to a setback often impacts your ability to make good decisions. This can have severe consequences, which may ultimately damage you.

For example, if your manager criticizes your work and asks you to start over, you might react to this setback angrily by threatening to resign. Or you might feel so nervous about your ability to perform satisfactorily in the future that you stall and can't move on from the setback.

Setbacks often make you feel stressed. They can set off an emotional response that clouds your judgment. However, your emotions should never dictate the decisions you make in life. You should base your decisions on logic, not emotion.

For example, you may react badly when your manager criticizes your work because you're worried you won't meet your deadline if you have to start all over again. Or you may react nervously because you're afraid you're not good enough.

Take note of your thoughts and feelings at work. When you experience a setback and feel stressed, ask yourself

Perseverance and Resilience

how you would view the setback if you were calmer. Always allow your initial reaction to subside before making a decision. In this way, your decision is more likely to be correct. And it's more likely to benefit you, rather than damage you.

So when you experience a setback, don't react immediately. Let your emotions die down before deciding what to do next.

Question

Which statement about emotional reactions is true?

Options:

1. People who decide based on their emotions are likely to make wiser decisions than people who leave emotions completely out of the decision-making process

2. When people mix their emotions with decision-making, they usually make bad decisions which can have severe consequences for them or even damage them

3. Human beings are emotional creatures, not robots, and they often make the best decisions when they're in an emotional frame of mind

Answer

Option 1: This option is incorrect. Emotional reactions to setbacks may be exaggerated or irrational. People who decide with their emotions are likely to make wrong decisions.

Option 2: This is the correct option. You should always allow your initial emotions to subside before making any decisions in life. In this way, your emotions won't dictate your decisions. And the decisions you make are more likely to be good ones.

Option 3: This option is incorrect. Although it's true that human beings are emotional, decisions should be based on logic, not emotion.

Expecting setbacks to occur

The second strategy you can use to develop your perseverance and resilience is to expect setbacks to occur in life and in work. In this way, you can be emotionally prepared for them. When you accept the inevitability of setbacks, you're more likely to regard them as opportunities to refocus on your goals, rather than as reasons to give up. When you adjust your expectations in this way, you're more likely to be successful.

In the workplace, things don't always go according to plan. So try to expect the unexpected. Prepare yourself mentally for unforeseen events, challenges, and outcomes – anything that might set you back or cause you to fail. If you can anticipate the setbacks that might occur, you'll be able to develop backup plans for coping with them. And you'll be more likely to remain calm and composed in difficult times and to find solutions to your problems.

Consider Judy's situation. She works as a programmer in a software company. She's just received a negative performance review from her manager. Judy hadn't fully examined her performance and didn't expect to get a negative review, so she isn't prepared for it emotionally. She feels shocked, humiliated, and depressed and starts to question her own abilities as a programmer. She wonders whether she should resign.

Judy's colleague, Marco, also received a negative performance review. But he knew he had made some serious errors at work recently, which might impact his review. So Marco is emotionally prepared for this setback when it occurs. He's determined to learn from the criticism he has received and to do better next time.

Judy and Marco face the same obstacle. By anticipating the setback and being emotionally prepared for it, Marco is in a better position to deal with the negative situation, learn from it, and move on.

When a setback does occur, you should regard it as a temporary obstacle that delays your progress. It can even be regarded as a partial success, in that it eliminates a course of action that doesn't work and allows you to focus on other ways of achieving your goals. Thomas Edison, for example, made hundreds of unsuccessful attempts to invent the light bulb. All those unsuccessful attempts weren't wasted, as they eventually resulted in a design that worked.

Question

Which of these attitudes would help you cope with a setback?

Options:

Perseverance and Resilience

1. "I didn't see that setback coming. I prefer to focus on positive outcomes rather than negative ones."

2. "I never feel defeated when I experience a setback. I regard setbacks as opportunities to refocus and

to explore other ways of reaching my goals."

3. "I don't expect life to be easy. I know I'm going to encounter difficulties and challenges along the way. They make me more determined."

4. "I usually regard setbacks as reasons to give up. If I can't do something well the first time, I'm obviously a failure."

Answer

Option 1: This option is incorrect. You should always expect the unexpected. Prepare yourself mentally for anything that might set you back or cause you to fail. If you can anticipate the setbacks that might occur, you'll be able to develop backup plans for coping with them.

Option 2: This option is correct. You should regard setbacks as opportunities to refocus on your goals, rather than as reasons to give up. You can even regard them as partial successes, in that they eliminate options that don't work.

Option 3: This option is correct. Things don't always go according to plan. If you adjust your expectations by accepting the inevitability of setbacks, you're more likely to be successful.

Option 4: This option is incorrect. When a setback does occur, you should regard it as a temporary obstacle that delays your forward progress. It doesn't mean you've been defeated or that you're a failure.

Viewing setbacks as opportunities

Viewing setbacks as opportunities

The third strategy you can use to develop your perseverance and resilience is to regard setbacks as opportunities for growth, change, and success rather than as insurmountable problems or proof that you're a failure. To do this, you should change your perspective on setbacks, so you don't interpret them in a defeatist way.

If you're a perseverant, resilient person, you regard setbacks as temporary glitches on the road to success. You aren't discouraged when you encounter a setback. You realize that a setback won't make a project fail – it's your response to the setback that does that. So when confronted with adversity, you tend to rise to the challenge and focus on overcoming the setback. You know you'll become closer than ever to reaching your goal.

Perseverance and Resilience

You can learn something positive from negative situations. In fact, mistakes and setbacks play an important role in your learning process. For example, you can learn a great deal by experimenting, by taking risks, by figuring out what went wrong, and by resolving to do better next time. So setbacks should be regarded as opportunities for learning and growth, instead of triggers for disappointment and self-doubt. You should ask yourself what you can learn after experiencing a setback.

You may have learned, among other things, that it's unwise to engage in black-and-white thinking about setbacks. Usually, situations aren't either perfect or a disaster. So you should avoid catastrophizing – or magnifying the effects of a setback. If you tend to blow events out of proportion, look for evidence that contradicts your way of thinking. For example, look for evidence that proves you're good at your job. And focus on positive steps you can take to deal with the situation.

Consider this situation. Carol is a manager in a software company, where she manages a small team of programmers. She has just experienced a major setback. Her star performer, Roberta, has unexpectedly resigned. Without the positive influence of Roberta, she's afraid that the productivity of the rest of the team will decrease. She's also worried that the other team members don't have the necessary skill and dedication required to get the important project they're working on completed on time.

Follow along as Carol discusses the setback with her colleague, Hassan.

Hassan: I heard Roberta has just resigned. You must be devastated. She's always been so reliable and dedicated. How will your team cope without her?

Hassan is concerned.

Carol: Well, I don't mind admitting that I felt angry when Roberta told me she was leaving. I mean, we've worked closely together for years and she never even hinted that she was considering leaving.

Carol is frustrated.

Hassan: I can understand your point of view. I'm sure I'd have felt the same way.

Hassan is understanding.

Carol: I was shocked by the news and the stress really clouded my judgment. I almost told her to clear her desk right away and leave the building! But I quickly calmed down and got things in perspective. We shook hands and I wished her well. And I'm going to organize a small farewell party for her at the end of the week.

Carol is calm.

Hassan: You dealt with the situation perfectly. Roberta deserves our good wishes. After all, she's done nothing wrong. And she helped to make this company the success it is today.

Hassan is positive.

Carol: Exactly. To be honest, I'd always anticipated that someone as talented as Roberta might be headhunted by one of our competitors one day. I always build extra time into our schedules in case of resignations or illness. I'm hoping this will allow the team to cope in Roberta's absence, to learn new skills, and to get back on track.

Carol is pleased.

Hassan: That's good thinking. I think I might do something similar myself. It makes sense to expect the unexpected.

Hassan is thoughtful.

Perseverance and Resilience

Carol: I also think Roberta's departure is the perfect opportunity to promote Sarah to team lead. She's been doing great work recently and I'm sure she'd relish the challenge of taking on some extra responsibilities. I realize I can depend on her to lead the team through the transition ahead.
Carol is happy.
Hassan: Sounds like you have everything under control, Carol! I wish I were as good at coping with setbacks as you are.
Hassan is good humored.

Carol experiences a major setback when her top performer resigns. But she quickly adopts strategies that draw on her perseverance and resilience and help her to cope with the setback. For example, she avoids having an exaggerated emotional response to Roberta's resignation by keeping things in perspective. And she doesn't let her emotions dictate how she behaves toward Roberta.

She also accepts that setbacks are an inevitable part of life. So she prepares herself mentally by developing contingency plans, which help her cope with Roberta's resignation.

Carol also views the setback as an opportunity to promote another team member, rather than as an excuse to fall apart. In this way, Carol displays her perseverance and resilience and copes well with the difficult situation she finds herself in.

Case Study: Question 1 of 2
Scenario
For your convenience, the case study is repeated with each question.

Taku works as a salesperson for a company that manufactures medical equipment. He's feeling stressed. He has just received an e-mail from the management committee of the largest hospital in the area – which is Taku's most important client.

Apparently, the hospital managers feel they have been taken for granted by Taku. They don't feel appreciated or cared for during their dealings with him. As a result, the managers won't be renewing the hospital's contract with Taku's company.

Taku knows he's to blame for this situation. He devoted all his energy to winning new customers, instead of nurturing existing clients. He failed to keep in touch with his key client on a regular basis and didn't provide the hospital managers with the personal service they deserved. Taku is humiliated and starts to panic. He knows the loss of this contract will negatively impact his company's balance sheet and that his job may be at risk.

Help Taku respond to this setback with perseverance and resilience by answering the questions in order.

Question

How should Taku respond to the setback initially?

Options:

1. Shout at his junior colleagues and blame them for not alerting him that the contract might be in jeopardy

2. Walk into the managing director's office, state that he's a total failure, and resign immediately

3. Allow his feelings of stress and humiliation to subside before making any decision about what to do next

4. Realize it's also possible the contract isn't being renewed because the hospital has found a cheaper supplier

5. Understand that his feelings of stress and humiliation are probably exaggerated

6. Admit his perspective is clouded by his emotions, so any actions he takes won't be driven by logic

Answer

Option 1: This option is incorrect. Taku should ensure his emotions don't control his actions. By shouting at his colleagues and blaming them for what's happened, he fails to understand and master the negative emotions he's feeling.

Option 2: This option is incorrect. By stating that he's a failure and opting to resign, Taku shows he's acting while under the influence of negative emotions. This clearly impacts his ability to make good decisions. He's displaying an irrational or exaggerated emotional response to the setback he has experienced, which is likely to damage him.

Option 3: This option is correct. Taku is wise to allow his initial reaction to subside before making a decision about what to do next. In this way, his decision is more likely to be correct. When you experience a setback and feel stressed, it's always best to ask yourself how you would view the setback if you were calmer.

Option 4: This option is correct. Although Taku knows he's made mistakes, he should also consider other reasons why the contract may not have been renewed. Often, the reason you fail has little to do with you and more to do with other people or external forces. So your initial emotional reaction may be exaggerated or irrational.

Option 5: This option is correct. Taku knows he should control and master the negative emotions he feels when he suffers a setback. He realizes these emotions may be exaggerated or irrational. And he may feel differently about the situation when his negative feelings subside and he regains his composure.

Option 6: This option is correct. Taku knows that it's dangerous to allow his emotions to rule his decision-making or hijack his perspective. By understanding where his emotional responses come from, he can control them. As a result, his future decisions and actions will be driven by logic, not emotion.

Case Study: Question 2 of 2

How can Taku display his perseverance and resilience as he attempts to deal with this setback?

Options:

1. Taku decides it's best to remain calm because, as a salesperson, he's prepared to lose and gain business

2. Taku opts to immediately implement his backup plan for winning back dissatisfied customers

3. Taku accepts that the loss of his most important customer means it will be impossible for him to reach his sales targets

4. Taku feels he has learned an important lesson about the necessity of ensuring that customers feel valued

5. Taku realizes he can win other contracts in the future, which may be even more lucrative than the one he's lost

6. Taku decides the hospital contract is too demanding, so he's not going to make any effort to win it back

Answer

Option 1: This option is correct. Taku expects setbacks to occur in life and in work. So he prepares himself mentally for unforeseen events, challenges, and outcomes – anything that might set him back or cause him to fail.

Perseverance and Resilience

Option 2: This option is correct. Taku is able to anticipate the setbacks that might occur at work. So he's able to develop backup plans for coping with them. This helps him to remain calm and composed in difficult times and to find solutions to his problems.

Option 3: This option is incorrect. Taku should regard the setback he has experienced as a temporary obstacle that delays his forward progress. He should look for ways of dealing with the crisis, instead of admitting defeat.

Option 4: This option is correct. Taku learns something positive from the negative situation he finds himself in. Setbacks should be regarded as opportunities for learning and growth, instead of triggers for disappointment and self-doubt.

Option 5: This option is correct. Taku avoids catastrophizing the setback and magnifying its effects. He knows it's unwise to engage in black-and-white thinking. The situation is neither perfect nor a complete disaster. It's better to focus on possible solutions.

Option 6: This option is incorrect. When confronted with adversity, Taku should rise to the challenge and focus on overcoming the setback. He shouldn't be discouraged or interpret the setback in a defeatist way. It's better to regard the setback as an opportunity for change and growth.

CHAPTER 2 - Achieving Goals through Perseverance and Resilience

CHAPTER 2 - Achieving Goals through Perseverance and Resilience

    Section 1 - Perseverance, Resilience, and Goal Setting
    Section 2 - Anticipating Obstacles
    Section 3 - Overcoming Obstacles

Section 1 - Perseverance, Resilience, and Goal Setting

Section 1 - Perseverance, Resilience, and Goal Setting

Setbacks and obstacles are a normal part of life that you have to learn to deal with. While some people may become frustrated by these difficulties, others manage to persevere and overcome their problems. One reason for this may be because they have set a goal that inspires them.

To create an inspiring goal, you need to make sure that it's measurable by planning what steps you have to take to reach your goal. You should ensure that your targets are achievable so that you don't end up feeling frustrated by an unrealistic goal.

Your goal should also be purposeful so that you're committed to follow through with your plan and are energized by the challenge. And to make your goal more tangible, write your aims down in specific and well-defined terms.

Goals and perseverance

Goals and perseverance

In business, just as in life, there are setbacks and obstacles you have to overcome in order to move forward and succeed. While some people may give up or become demotivated, others manage to rise above these challenges. Why do some people find it easier to face adversity, and bounce back from setbacks than others? One possible reason may be because they have a goal that drives their perseverance and resilience.

Take Valerie, for example. She works as an executive at an advertising firm, and wants to become the head of her department within the next five years. To achieve this goal, she knows that she must demonstrate a consistent track record in reaching her sales targets. However, Valerie finds out that senior executives are cutting her department's marketing funds. This means she'll have far less money to promote her client's line of products, which may cause her to miss her sales targets.

Despite this obstacle, Valerie keeps her goal of becoming the head of the Sales Department in mind, and is determined not to let reduced funding hold her back. She first tries to market her client's product through an online promotion as it is cost effective. However, poor sales figures show that this approach isn't reaching her target audience.

She then comes up with another idea, and contacts one of her colleagues who is promoting another product category. She tells him that she plans to create an event to market both their products. She explains that if they pool their funds, they can cross-promote their products more effectively.

In spite of their reduced funding, both Valerie and her colleague manage to meet and exceed their sales quotas. The event is such a success, her strategy is used in other departments to cross-promote client products. This not only helps the company to increase its revenue, but also gives Valerie the self-assurance that she can overcome other problems that may arise in the future.

You may have noted that Valerie was able to overcome this obstacle by having the determination to reach her goal. By having a clear goal, Valerie was able to focus on what needed to be done, and kept moving forward to achieve her objectives.

Valerie also showed she had the motivation to continue striving for her goal. People often question their motivation when they encounter difficulties, and may abandon their goal altogether. That's why it's important to make sure that the goal you set is of value to you, and not because it sounds impressive.

And by overcoming a significant problem, Valerie built up her confidence, which will enable her to face other difficulties she may encounter. Confidence is an essential element of perseverance and resilience – being self-assured will help you to stay on target no matter what setback you face. This, in turn, also reinforces your determination and motivation.

You should keep in mind three steps that will help you to achieve your goal and persevere when you encounter obstacles or setbacks. First, you need to have an inspiring goal to help you to stay motivated. Second, you should anticipate obstacles that may arise so that you're adequately prepared to deal with them. And lastly, you must learn to overcome these obstacles so that your efforts to achieve your goal aren't undermined.

Question

How might you benefit from being able to use techniques of perseverance and resilience when trying to achieve your goal?

Options:

1. It may enable you to overcome setbacks that get in your way

2. You can put difficulties that may arise into better perspective

3. It will help you to prioritize and achieve goals set by your peers

4. You'll be better able to focus on your goal and become more determined

5. It enables you to gain the confidence required to achieve your goal

Perseverance and Resilience

6. You'll be able to achieve your goal with a minimal amount of effort

Answer

Option 1: This option is correct. People who achieve their goals do so not just because they have the right knowledge, but because they also have the determination to do so.

Option 2: This option is correct. Being resilient and confident can help you look past obstacles and see the bigger picture.

Option 3: This option is incorrect. Whenever you try to reach a goal, you should make sure that it is one that you are personally inspired by. Trying to pursue other people's goals may lead to a lack of motivation when facing major difficulties.

Option 4: This option is correct. Having a clearly defined goal can help you concentrate on the steps to reach that goal, and give you the incentive needed to follow through with your plans.

Option 5: This option is correct. Successfully overcoming a problem in the pursuit of your goal can give you courage and enthusiasm when facing other difficulties.

Option 6: This option is incorrect. Reaching a goal is rarely easy – it takes determination and persistence to overcome setbacks along the way.

Measurable goals

Measurable goals

The first step in the process of accomplishing a goal is to ensure that your goal is inspiring and clearly defined. Ideally, you should set a goal for yourself that requires you to grow and develop as you progress toward your objective. But remember that there's a fine line between a realistic goal that drives you to improve and an unattainable goal that can actually lead to frustration and demotivation. That's why you must put time into planning your goal in advance.

To drive your perseverance and resilience, and provide some direction, your goals should have certain characteristics. Effective goals should be "MAPS" – that is, they must be measurable, achievable, purposeful, and specific. "MAPS" goals can provide a framework for your efforts, and can help you to put obstacles and setbacks into perspective.

Perseverance and Resilience

The first characteristic of effective goals is that they're measurable. This means deciding how much you want to increase or decrease your targets by, and the date by which your goal should be accomplished.

Whatever your goal is, it should be expressed in clear and well-defined terms. For example, a poorly defined goal might be to reduce your company's expenditures, or to increase your knowledge. Instead, a more measurable business goal would be to reduce transportation costs by 10% over the next year. Or it could be to attend five sales conventions by the end of the year.

And to ensure your goal is still on track, you should measure your progress. For instance, if your aim is to increase your company's market share by 15% over the next two years, you could carry out a quarterly status review to see if you're hitting your target.

Consider Omar, a supervisor at a call center. Although Omar is happy with his current position, he would like to take on more responsibility, and to have a say in the direction his company takes.

He's aware that the only way he can be involved in the organization's strategy is to seek a managerial position. This is why he sets a goal for himself of becoming a call center teams manager within the year.

Question

Which examples are characteristic of measurable goals?

Options:

1. To increase customer satisfaction by ten points by the end of the next quarter

2. To improve employee productivity and overall morale levels

3. To become proficient at setting up electronic balance sheets within three months

4. To increase sales revenue from advertising over the next two years

Answer

Option 1: This option is correct. This goal is measurable as it details how much customer satisfaction ratings should increase by, as well as the date by which this should be accomplished.

Option 2: This option is incorrect. This statement is too vague, and doesn't provide any details about when and how this goal can be accomplished.

Option 3: This option is correct. This statement outlines exactly what the aim is and when this should be achieved.

Option 4: This option is incorrect. While this goal does provide a time line, it doesn't specify how much the company should increase its sales revenue by.

Achievable goals

Achievable goals

Another feature of effective goals is that they are achievable. Make sure that whatever goal you set for yourself is realistic so you don't end up feeling discouraged or frustrated if you're unable to reach this goal.

An achievable goal is one that will challenge your skills and abilities, but that is still within your control. For example, if you aim to introduce and train employees on a new product management system, it may be unrealistic to achieve this within one week. Instead, consider all the factors involved, and give yourself a reasonable chance for success.

While thinking big can be a positive aspect when setting out your goal, it's important not to let this undermine your efforts. One way of dealing with this is to break your goal down into smaller but significant milestones. To gauge your progress, you need to create shorter-term goals, which can be more easily evaluated.

For instance, doubling your company's revenue may be unrealistic if it's in the middle of an economic downturn, or if the company lacks the infrastructure to reach that target. However, you can break this goal down into subgoals, such as reaching a minimum of a 10% increase in revenue within the first quarter. Using this milestone, you can then judge whether your goal is still achievable, and adjust it accordingly.

Remember Omar? He has set a goal of becoming a call center teams manager at his company within the next year. Omar makes this an achievable goal by first informing his manager of his intention. They then create a plan together to work on some of Omar's weaknesses.

Omar's goal is also realistic as his manager can see that he's serious about it, and is able to review what Omar has learned.

And to ensure that he's making progress, Omar sets several targets for himself along the way, such as completing a project management course before the end of the year.

Question

Which of these goals do you think are achievable and realistic?

Options:

1. Miguel intends to make his startup company into the leading supplier of fashion accessories by the end of the year

2. Rita plans to develop her own web site to create an online presence for her company and increase sales by 10%

Perseverance and Resilience

3. Werner wants to increase his soft drinks company market share by 3% over the next two years

4. Nick plans to overhaul his company's manufacturing process by introducing a new QA program by the end of the month

Answer

Option 1: This option is incorrect. This goal may not be realistic because Miguel's company is new and might not have the infrastructure, relationships, and systems in place to overtake its competitors.

Option 2: This option is correct. Rita's goal is achievable because the design of a web site is within her control, and because she has set a realistic sales figure for her company.

Option 3: This option is correct. Werner's objective may be achievable as it sets a reasonable sales target, and provides a deadline that will enable his company to gauge its progress.

Option 4: This option is incorrect. Introducing a new QA process may require a lot of analysis, planning, and training, which might not be achievable within a one month deadline.

Purposeful goals

Purposeful goals

The next characteristic of effective goals is that they are purposeful. Whatever target you set for yourself, ensure that it's one that you're genuinely enthusiastic about – this will also help you to own and commit to your goal.

To make your goal more meaningful, visualize yourself reaching your goal. Imagining the positive end result of your efforts can help to motivate you even further. For example, if your goal is to improve your sales figures, you could picture yourself getting a well-earned bonus for your hard work. You might also see yourself getting recognition from your managers or colleagues. This technique can encourage you to persevere when facing obstacles to your goal.

Purposeful goals are relevant for you or your organization's requirements. When setting out your goal, consider the current realities and conditions of the business climate. Meaningful goals also challenge you to grow and develop. Challenges are there to excite and energize you. Try to adopt a goal that is possible but that you're not 100% sure you will attain. The uncertainty will motivate you to succeed.

Consider Omar again. Omar has chosen the goal of becoming a manager within his company, as it's relevant to his career progression. He wants to take on more responsibility, and this would be an ideal opportunity to outline his goals and ambitions.

Omar realizes that getting his promotion won't be an easy task. He knows that he'll need to develop personally and professionally. However, he's excited by the challenge of completing his project management course, and by the prospect of applying what he's learned.

And to motivate himself further, Omar tries to imagine the benefits of the position if he's successful. He recognizes that, besides increased financial rewards, he'll have a greater input into the teams' day-to- day activities, and he'll make a positive impact on their work routine.

Question

Joan owns a small marketing firm that's experiencing financial losses because of a downturn in the economy. Despite this, Joan sets a goal of returning to profitability within 12 months. She plans to achieve this by streamlining her company's administrative processes and by increasing contracts by 10%. While she realizes this will be problematic, she knows if successful, she'll be able to grow and expand her business even further.

Why is this a purposeful goal for Joan?

Options:

1. It's relevant to her company's current situation

2. Her goal is easily attainable
3. She has set a realistic deadline for herself
4. It will help to keep her motivated

Answer

Option 1: This option is correct. Having a relevant goal that takes into account current market realities is essential when addressing an organization's needs.

Option 2: This option is incorrect. While it's important to have a goal that is achievable, ideally a goal should challenge and energize people, and force them to develop personally and professionally.

Option 3: This option is incorrect. Although a measurable aspect such as a deadline is critical to a goal's success, it shouldn't be used as a motivational tool. The purpose of Joan's goal should be the end result or benefits of achieving the goal.

Option 4: This option is correct. Joan recognizes that there will be several benefits of achieving her goal, which help to maintain her commitment.

Specific goals

Specific goals
The final attribute of effective goals is that they are specific. To keep your efforts on track, you need to document your goals in clear terms, and explain how you intend to achieve them.

While it's important to visualize what you want to achieve, you should also write down your goals and specific methods of accomplishing them. Once you have set your goal down in writing, your idea will become more concrete.

Writing your goal down also forces you to become more specific, and to clearly define what your goals are. Putting your goal down in writing enables you to think about other aspects of your goal, such as subgoals, or important milestones.

You should also document your progress, and keep a report to remind yourself of your efforts so far if faced with serious setbacks. This can help you stay committed and motivated to overcome future obstacles.

Take Omar, for example. He knows that he'll face a lot of difficulties, as advancement within his company can be difficult to achieve, and requires a proven track record.

To prove his ability, Omar writes out a weekly report of what skills he has learned, and presents it to his manager. In his report, he also documents problems he has encountered, and steps he has taken to resolve them.

Question

What are the benefits of documenting your progress toward your end goal?

Options:

1. It gives a sense of reality to your goal
2. It enables you to anticipate potential problems
3. It can motivate you to overcome obstacles
4. It shows others that you're serious about your goal

Answer

Option 1: This option is correct. Writing the things you want to achieve down on paper enables you to create a concrete plan of action.

Option 2: This option is incorrect. Writing your progress down may not help you to foresee future obstacles, but can help you to stay motivated if they do arise.

Option 3: This option is correct. By seeing how far you've progressed, you're less likely to give up at the first sign of trouble.

Option 4: This option is incorrect. The aim of writing your goal down is to make your dream more tangible, not to impress others.

Perseverance and Resilience

Consider Sandra, a team leader at an online travel agency. Recently, bookings at her company have been falling significantly. Senior executives have decided to set up an incentives program to boost sales, and will offer the team with the most bookings a free return flight to any destination. Sandra decides to set a goal of increasing her team's sales by 50% by the end of the quarter to win the team award.

To achieve this goal, Sandra creates a chart to document her team members' progress, which she updates frequently to show their current sales figures. However, although Sandra's team members are motivated by the bonus program, they are unable to reach their set target and completely lose track along the way. They soon realize that they're unlikely to attain their goal, and frustration begins to set in.

In the previous example, Sandra set a purposeful goal, as it outlined a positive end result for her team members and would help to motivate them. She also documented her goal, and kept a record of her team members' progress.

However, Sandra's goal was ineffective, as it failed to outline in measurable terms what her team should achieve. To make her goal more measurable, Sandra should have broken it down into smaller subgoals, such as to improve her team members' phone skills or product knowledge.

And Sandra's goal, while not impossible, was unrealistic. As her company was already experiencing a drop in bookings, setting a target of a 50% increase within the quarter would have been difficult to achieve. For example, a more realistic target of 10 to 15% would still offer her team members a challenge, but one less likely to cause frustration.

Case Study: Question 1 of 2
Scenario

Tyrone works as a regional manager at a freight transport company, and wants to impress senior managers by implementing a cost-savings program. Although his company is the leading freight transport firm in the industry, Tyrone sets a goal of saving 5% in expenditure within two years. To achieve this, he plans to conduct quarterly office supply and energy utility audits. He also sets a milestone of reaching a 2% reduction by the end of the first year.

After a few months, Tyrone is unsure if his plan is working, as he hasn't kept track of savings in each of the company's departments. He soon abandons his goal, as he realizes that it won't have a significant impact on the company's profitability.

Examine Tyrone's goal and answer the following questions in order.

Question

Which of these statements accurately describe Tyrone's goal?

Options:

1. Tyrone has the drive and ambition to reduce savings in his company
2. He has planned some specific methods to cut costs
3. He is keeping an accurate record to log his progress
4. Tyrone has outlined a reasonable target and schedule

Answer

Option 1: This option is incorrect. Although he has established a clear goal, Tyrone hasn't identified a purposeful reward his organization should strive for. And as his aim is to impress his bosses, he may not be personally motivated by the challenge.

Option 2: This option is correct. Tyrone has set a measurable goal by outlining some of the processes, such as supply audits, his organization can use to cut costs.

Option 3: This option is incorrect. To help make his targets more tangible, Tyrone should have written his goal down and documented his progress.

Option 4: This option is correct. Tyrone has set a realistic milestone, which gives him and his organization a better chance of achieving his goal.

Case Study: Question 2 of 2

What actions do you think Tyrone could take to make his goal more effective?

Options:

1. He could push himself harder by trying to expand his company's business into another market

2. He could keep a report of how much his company has reduced costs by

3. He could try to cut costs by 25% within the next month to motivate himself further

4. He could announce his goal to his colleagues to demonstrate his strategic perspective

Answer

Option 1: This option is correct. Setting a more difficult but achievable target might help to keep Tyrone energized.

Option 2: This option is correct. Tyrone can keep track of his progress by documenting how closely he is sticking to his targets. This would also help to keep him motivated when faced with setbacks.

Option 3: This option is incorrect. This target might not be realistic, and may be outside of Tyrone's control.

Option 4: This option is incorrect. The aim of Tyrone's goal shouldn't be to impress others but to achieve something of value for himself and his company.

Section 2 - Anticipating Obstacles
Section 2 - Anticipating Obstacles

A common error people make when planning goals is to neglect to anticipate possible obstacles. An unforeseen challenge can sometimes stop people in their tracks, and lead to disappointment or frustration.

To overcome these obstacles, you should first identify all the possible problems that you may have to face. Once you've listed these problems, you categorize them as either major or minor, which helps to prioritize tasks that are urgent or important. Having narrowed the scope of possible obstacles, you need to identify the key obstacle you must overcome.

Anticipating problems

Anticipating problems

Having an inspiring goal is essential in keeping you motivated, and helping you to follow through with your plans. But what happens if you come up against an unforeseen barrier between you and your goal? Many people may become frustrated or feel overwhelmed. Remember that with any goal, there will always be some obstacles that you'll need to overcome in order to succeed. That's why you must anticipate these obstacles and prepare for them in advance.

Persevering and being resilient in order to achieve your goal involves recognizing and preparing for problems that may arise. To help you overcome any obstacles you encounter, you first need to list all the potential problems that you're likely to face. Next, you have to categorize and prioritize these potential obstacles. And lastly, you must identify the key obstacle that may hinder your success as you strive for your goal.

Defining potential obstacles allows you to put pitfalls into perspective, and enables you to develop strategies to overcome them. And, although there may still be some unexpected challenges on your path toward your goal, focusing on the main issues will help to ensure that your plans stay on track.

Question

Put the three steps to anticipating obstacles in the correct order.

Options:

A. List potential problems
B. Categorize and prioritize obstacles
C. Identify key obstacle

Answer

List potential problems is ranked the first step. The first step when preparing for obstacles to your goal is to make a list of all the problems that you're likely to encounter.

Categorize and prioritize obstacles is ranked the second step. The second step when anticipating obstacles is to rank them according to their level of importance or urgency.

Identify key obstacle is ranked the third step. The last step when anticipating obstacles is to pinpoint what you consider to be the main issue that needs to be addressed.

Listing potential problems

Listing potential problems

The first step when anticipating obstacles is to list all the potential problems that you might encounter. When creating your list, make sure that any hindrances you outline are relative to your goal. Remember that what may be an obstacle for one goal might not have a substantive impact on another. While every goal is different and will have its particular challenges, there are three common types of obstacles that you should bear in mind: situational, interpersonal, and personal.

Situational

When considering your goal, try to take into account how your organization's situation or current environment may affect your success.

For example, if your goal is to expand your business into another market, you could look into environmental factors such as the receptivity of customers in that market to your product or service.

You might also take into account how larger situational problems such as a downturn in the global market may impact your goal.

Interpersonal

Interpersonal problems involve difficulties in relationships with other people. They often relate to miscommunications, or a lack of communication with other stakeholders or team members. You may also have to deal with people who don't share your enthusiasm for your goal, and aren't motivated to help you along the way.

For instance, if you want to get promoted to a managerial position, you may need to consider which people will have the time and motivation to give you the advice and experience you need to achieve this.

Personal

Obstacles may often involve your own ability to handle the targets you've set for yourself. You may lack the skills necessary to achieve your goal, or be unable to manage your time effectively.

If your goal is to improve your customer satisfaction ratings, for example, you might need to think about your own call-handling techniques and problem-solving skills.

Consider Andrew, a regional manager at a telecommunications company. He has set a goal for himself of moving one of his company's call center operations abroad by the end of the year. To ensure his plan flows smoothly, Andrew first looks into situational problems, such as the cost of building a new office block to accommodate employees.

Andrew then thinks about potential communication difficulties, as he knows that the time zone of the planned office is several hours behind that of headquarters.

He also considers the scope of his goal to find out if it's realistic to relocate his company's office overseas within the deadline he has set for himself.

Question

Wendy is a sales executive at an electronics retail company. She's planning to improve sales by offering customers the ability to purchase goods online by the end of the next quarter.

What are the potential obstacles to the success of Wendy's goal?

Options:

1. Customers may not consider the company's products good value for money

2. The company's servers may not be able to handle large volumes of purchases

3. Customer service staff might be unwilling to take on the extra workload

4. Customers may prefer to buy her company's products in-store rather than online

Answer

Option 1: This option is incorrect. The aim of Wendy's goal is to ensure that her company's products are available for purchase online. The possibility that customers may find her company's products poor value for money will have little impact on this goal.

Option 2: This option is correct. A computer hardware glitch is a situational problem that may have a significant impact on Wendy's goal.

Option 3: This option is correct. An interpersonal problem such as a lack of cooperation or motivation on the part of employees could present a serious setback to Wendy's goal.

Option 4: This option is incorrect. As the customers' purchasing preferences will still lead to sales, this won't affect Wendy's goal.

Categorizing and prioritizing obstacles

Categorizing and prioritizing obstacles

The next step when anticipating problems is to categorize and prioritize obstacles. It's crucial to divide potential obstacles into major and minor problems to help you find out which tasks are most important, and which need to be carried out urgently. And while you can't foresee everything, you need to be aware of how probable certain obstacles are, and the impact they could have.

Major obstacles are issues that may require considerable planning, skills, or resources. They may also be time consuming, so they should be resolved quickly if you have an important deadline to reach.

They are also the issues that are critical to the success of your goal. They must be addressed before you can move on and deal with other less important tasks.

Perseverance and Resilience

For example, issues such as the resignation of key team members, loss of investors, or a change in corporate direction may all have a huge impact on your goal.

Minor obstacles, on the other hand, are generally easier tasks that may not require your immediate attention.

They're also the problems that can be addressed as and when the opportunity arises. However, it's important to keep a list of minor obstacles and ensure that they don't become a significant barrier if left unresolved.

Examples of minor obstacles to achieving a goal might include deciding what type of software to use for a project, or finding a training course to take to improve your skills.

Consider Andrew again. He's planning the relocation of a call center office, and has come up with a number of obstacles that may hinder the success of this move. In his list, he outlines funding problems, as his company recently suffered some financial losses.

He considers communication difficulties between offices located in different overseas areas, and training requirements for new recruits in the planned office. Andrew then looks into tax compliance issues in the overseas location, as well as the need for an effective communications plan to inform employees about his proposal.

Andrew decides that the funding and tax compliance issues are major issues that need to be addressed urgently for the plan to be successful. He also believes that the training and communications problems are less urgent and can be resolved at a later stage in the planning process.

Question

Taku is a manager at an online gourmet food company, and plans to introduce a new range of organic products within the next year. Match the obstacles Taku has listed to their corresponding categories. Each category may match to more than one obstacle.

Options:

A. Develop a product that complies with food regulations

B. Find people to perform taste testing

C. Find suppliers and distributors for the new product

D. Work out time lines relating to delivery

Targets:

1. Major obstacles
2. Minor obstacles

Answer

Developing a product that meets food standards, as well as finding suppliers and distributors, are two major obstacles that may be critical to the success of Taku's goal. These may be time-consuming tasks that require much planning and resources, and so should be prioritized.

Working out time lines relating to delivery and performing taste testing are tasks that may not require Taku's immediate attention, and so don't have be prioritized.

Identifying the key obstacle

The final step when anticipating problems is to identify the key obstacle. Although you may have to face several different problems, there's usually one crucial issue you need to resolve in order to progress toward your goal.

Identifying the key obstacle to your goal is essential, as you may not be able to complete other tasks without tackling the main problem.

However, keep in mind that although this may not be the most difficult issue to resolve, it may be the most time consuming, and the one that requires most energy.

Remember Andrew? He's narrowed down major obstacles to his goal to funding and tax compliance issues. He now considers which of these obstacles will have the greatest impact on his goal.

Andrew decides to focus on the problem of a potential lack of funding. He realizes that if his organization needs to cut expenditures, his goal of opening an overseas office may be jeopardized.

He also recognizes that finding the funds to carry out his goal may be a lengthy process, and one that will affect his ability to overcome his other obstacles.

Question

Nancy is a project manager at an IT firm, and plans to reduce office supply costs by 10% by the end of the year. She has narrowed down her obstacles to three main issues.

Which of these obstacles do you think represents the key obstacle to Nancy's goal?

Options:

1. Tackling wasteful usage of specific office supplies
2. Negotiating supplier rates to reduce prices of office items
3. Creating a detailed audit of supply costs and usage

Answer

Option 1: This option is incorrect. Nancy first needs to create an audit of office supplies to find out where they are being wasted.

Option 2: This option is incorrect. To find out how much suppliers are currently charging, Nancy would first need to carry out an audit, which would help her find out what office items are most in demand.

Option 3: This is the correct option. To find out where her company needs to cut costs, Nancy first needs to find out how much the company is currently spending on its supplies. This will help her to determine where supplies are being wasted and to see where supplies rates may be reduced.

Section 3 - Overcoming Obstacles
Section 3 - Overcoming Obstacles

How to overcome obstacles

How to overcome obstacles

Persevering to achieve your goal involves creating an inspiring goal for yourself and anticipating potential obstacles along the way. But being truly resilient means actually overcoming obstacles when they arise. Although you may have planned your goal and prepared for possible obstacles, finding the determination to overcome major problems is often the most difficult aspect of achieving your goal.

There are four key steps you should keep in mind to overcome major obstacles. First, you need to recognize how you react to obstacles so you can deal with them more effectively, and understand what the root cause is. Second, you must reaffirm your abilities and stay positive. The third step is to refocus on your goal and learn from your experience. And lastly, you must resume with an alternative plan and move forward with confidence.

Perseverance and Resilience

Obstacles are what make goals challenging and motivating. But without the right attitude they can seem like insurmountable barriers to your goal.

However, by staying positive, you can learn from your mistakes and focus your energy on what you can control.

Question

Put the four steps for overcoming obstacles in the correct order.

Options:

A. Recognize
B. Reaffirm
C. Refocus
D. Resume

Answer

Recognize is ranked the first step. You first need to understand what caused the problem, and not take the obstacle personally.

Reaffirm is ranked the second step. Second, you should control your response to the obstacle, and keep a positive attitude about your abilities.

Refocus is ranked the third step. Third, you must learn from the lesson and develop or change your plan.

Resume is ranked the fourth step. Finally, you need to take action while keeping your goal in sight.

Recognize the obstacle

Recognize the obstacle

The first step when trying to overcome an obstacle is to recognize your own reaction to the problem. People can often become flustered when faced with a serious obstacle, and blame themselves for the mistake. But it's important to view mistakes as opportunities to grow and learn.

If you encounter an obstacle, step back from the situation to get a better perspective. Taking the problem personally may cloud your judgment, so try to understand how you usually interpret difficulties. Avoid blaming others or making excuses, and try to define the obstacle clearly. And be honest about what has happened – ignoring or downplaying the obstacle may only intensify its impact.

Take Manuel for example. He's a project manager at a company that manufactures entertainment systems. His company is introducing a new range of game consoles, which have been preordered by a large number of electronics retailers.

With his products packed and ready for delivery, Manuel realizes that the packages won't fit into the delivery trucks. He discovers that the shape and size of the boxes make it difficult to pack them side by side in the truck.

Manuel also sees that the trucks are much smaller than he had anticipated. He realizes that the shipping company must have misunderstood his order.

Although Manuel is upset that his delivery may be delayed, he doesn't let this overwhelm him. Instead, he tries to define the problem, and aims to understand its root cause.

He finds out that there was a miscommunication with the shipping company, as he failed to detail what types of trucks were needed.

Having considered the cause of the problem, he also looks at how this may impact his delivery times. He knows that many of the retailers are awaiting delivery today, so it's vital to resolve the issue to avoid affecting sales of his company's product.

Question

Which examples demonstrate effective recognition and understanding of obstacles?

Options:

1. Stan realizes he didn't take different time zones into account when planning his team's schedule, which caused it to miss its deadline

2. Gloria tries to figure out how an increase in production costs will affect her goal to reduce her company's expenditure

3. Rose blames her lack of experience in project management as the main reason she has missed her deadline

4. Nicholas focuses on past failures and mistakes he might have made after failing to get promoted to a managerial position

Answer

Option 1: This option is correct. Stan clearly defines the root cause of his obstacle.

Option 2: This option is correct. Gloria focuses on what impact the obstacle might have rather than taking the bad news to heart.

Option 3: This option is incorrect. Instead of focusing on her failings, Rose should try to recognize how she usually reacts to obstacles.

Option 4: This option is incorrect. Nicholas shouldn't take this obstacle personally. He could try to see this obstacle more objectively to see if there were any external reasons why he didn't get his desired position.

Reaffirm your abilities

Reaffirm your abilities

The second step to overcome an obstacle is to reaffirm your abilities. Although your plan may not have worked out as you had intended, you should maintain a positive attitude about yourself and your skills and control any negative reactions.

When faced with a major obstacle, some people may overemphasize their mistakes, and make negative or generalized statements such as "I can't do anything right." That's why you need to control your initial response. By challenging these pessimistic beliefs and focusing on your successes so far, you can remain optimistic about the outcome of your efforts. Remember that one failure doesn't mean your goal is no longer valid or possible.

Remember Manuel? He's frustrated that after so many months of research and development, his goal of releasing the consoles on time has nearly been ruined by not planning the shipments properly.

However, he understands that he shouldn't dwell on this obstacle. Instead, he focuses on the hard work he and his team members have put in during the project. And he thinks of the time and effort to bring the game consoles from the concept stage to final development.

Manuel also realizes that he has had to use his problem-solving skills to get to this stage. He knows that he can use this ability to find a way around this current obstacle.

Question

Which examples demonstrate a reaffirming attitude to an obstacle?

Options:

1. Maria decides that she should seek a new position within the company after failing to reach her sales target for the month

2. Steven tries to focus on recommendations from previous employers after he fails to get his desired promotion

3. Ayana believes that she hasn't managed her time properly in order to complete her project and decides to reconsider her goal

4. Liz is frustrated by her team's low sales figures but congratulates the team members on their high customer satisfaction ratings

Answer

Option 1: This option is incorrect. Maria should try to reaffirm her abilities in sales and not let her failure sidetrack her goal.

Perseverance and Resilience

Option 2: This option is correct. By reaffirming his abilities, Steven can build up his self-confidence and try for promotion again in the future.

Option 3: This option is incorrect. Ayana should try to control her initial reaction to the obstacle – this may help her to stay motivated and not let self doubts overwhelm her.

Option 4: This option is correct. It's important to highlight what Liz's team has done right so that it can move forward with confidence and carry on with its targets.

Refocus on your goal

Refocus on your goal

The next step to overcome an obstacle is to refocus on your goal. Once you've maintained a positive attitude and found out the root cause of your obstacle, you can try to work out a new plan to achieve your goal.

To refocus your goal and overcome obstacles, you first need to learn from the lesson. It's important to capitalize on your mistake or oversight so that you don't repeat it in the future. For example, you could brainstorm ideas with colleagues to find an alternative solution. When brainstorming ideas, you should start by focusing on one clearly defined problem. You could then identify strategies or tactics that have worked in the past, and adapt them to your current situation.

In order to achieve your ultimate objective, you may also have to change some of your key milestones or targets. Remember that changing some aspects of your goal is better than abandoning it altogether.

For example, if your goal is to reduce company's expenditures by 10% by the end of the year, you could change either your deadline or your target to ensure that your company does actually reduce spending.

Consider Manuel again. He's reviewed the communication error that lead to the problem with his packaged products. Having consulted with some of his colleagues, he now realizes that other smaller trucks may be on their way to pick up the shipment of game consoles.

He also knows that he'll have to deal with the trucks that are currently waiting to pick up their shipment. Manuel asks some of his colleagues in the shipping yard if the packaging methods can be changed, and if certain materials can be removed.

Question

Which examples demonstrate effective methods of refocusing on goals?

Options:

1. Bernadette gets her team to refine her original plan of increasing her department's revenue by the year end

2. Tim decides to maintain his current plan of action despite failing to get a promotion after his second unsuccessful interview

3. Bhadrak focuses on changing his goal of increasing his company's market share after another company introduces a similar product

4. Loretta considers how her company can use a previous marketing campaign to improve sales of one of its products

Answer

Option 1: This option is correct. Finding an alternative means of reaching a goal is an essential part of persevering in the face of obstacles.

Option 2: This option is incorrect. It's important to learn lessons from previous mistakes, and to use past experience to develop new ideas or plans.

Option 3: This option is incorrect. Instead of trying to change his goal, Bhadrak should see if there are other methods of increasing his company's market share.

Option 4: This option is correct. Persevering in the face of obstacles involves learning from previous experiences and applying ideas to new situations.

Resume with a new plan

Resume with a new plan

The final step to overcome obstacles is to resume with an alternative plan. Being resilient often means coming up with a new plan of action to achieve your ultimate goal.

When resuming with a new plan of action, try to focus on the things you can actually control. Some factors, such as economic downturns, are outside of your control. Devoting your efforts to uncontrollable situations is a waste of your time and energy.

There are some factors that you can influence, even though you can't control them. For example, suppose your team members are demotivated. Although you can't tell them to be enthusiastic, you could create a more supportive environment for them, or devise a new incentives scheme.

Then there are the factors that are within your control. For instance, although you may view a lack of knowledge as an obstacle to your goal, you can choose to learn by taking a training course, or by asking someone to help you.

Once you've identified what's within your control, you have to take decisive action. Although you may be facing overwhelming obstacles, you need to assert your vision through your new plan of action. While your plan may involve changing your approach, milestones, or targets, it should stay true to your end goal. And remember to focus on your strengths. By emphasizing your skills and talents, you'll be better able to move forward with confidence.

Remember Manuel? He knows that while he can't do anything about the size of the trucks, he can control the packing methods. He gets help from some of the employees in the Shipping Department to alter the packing materials so that the game consoles fit better into the trucks.

He also realizes that he must stop the situation from getting worse by calling the trucking company and stopping more wrong trucks from arriving. And he makes sure to specify which trucks he needs to deliver his products on time.

Question

Which examples demonstrate a plan of action being implemented to achieve a goal?

Options:

1. After failing to get a promotion to a managerial position, Betty decides to complete a course in project management

2. Roy outlines a new marketing campaign to his team members after they fail to reach their sales target for the month

Perseverance and Resilience

3. Lucy reviews the economic downturn and its effect on sales in the pharmaceutical industry, as she's falling short of her quarterly target

4. Thomas decides to carry out a feasibility study to see if his plan to reduce company expenditure is still relevant

Answer

Option 1: This option is correct. Betty tries to overcome her obstacle by controlling an aspect that may have caused her to not get the promotion she wanted.

Option 2: This option is correct. Creating a new plan of action is an effective way of overcoming obstacles and keeping a goal in sight.

Option 3: This option is incorrect. While it's important to understand the root cause of her problem, Lucy should focus on the things she can control.

Option 4: This option is incorrect. Perseverance and resilience are pointless if there is no action, which is why Thomas should try to move forward with his plan.

Consider Elaine. She's a team leader at a sportswear manufacturing company that is introducing a new range of sports equipment. She has set a target of achieving a 10% share of the market by the end of the year. However, revenue from the new equipment remains consistently low, and sales figures show that her company is set for a 3% market share.

Although the sales figures are disappointing, Elaine knows from previous experience that new products can often perform poorly at the start. She points this out to her team members, telling them that this is no reflection on their skills or abilities, and that sales will eventually pick up. She's also confident that the product will find a niche market, and that her team should continue with their current marketing campaign.

By the end of the next quarter, however, sales figures are down even further. Elaine decides to look into the issue, and after consulting with several retailers, finds that a rival company has released a similar product at a lower price.

She knows that her company has lost a lot of ground to its main competitors, and that it needs to make some drastic changes to its marketing campaign to improve sales.

In the previous example, Elaine does well by not letting self-defeating assumptions affect her motivation to improve sales of her company's product. She remains positive, and tries to inspire motivation in her team members.

However, Elaine downplays the impact of the obstacle, and assumes that sales will improve without fully understanding the root cause of the problem.

And although she eventually learns from her experience, Elaine should have come up with an alternative plan earlier. This may have helped her company regain some of the market share lost to its main rivals.

Case Study: Question 1 of 2
Scenario

Simon has given up his job at a publishing company to run his own monthly advertisement publication. He aims to write articles of local interest, and to sell advertising space for local businesses and services.

However, after a number of months, Simon is struggling to find clients willing to advertise in his publication. After contacting businesses in the area, he realizes that most of the companies cannot afford his rates, or have already found alternative advertising sources.

Simon is disappointed by the news, and regrets leaving his previous position. Believing that his publication has little chance of taking off, he focuses on finding another position similar to his previous job.

Examine Simon's goal and answer the following questions in order.

Question

To overcome this major obstacle to his goal, Simon must first recognize what went wrong, and see the situation for what it really is.

Which statement accurately aligns with Simon's goal?

Options:

1. He realizes what his real strengths and talents are

2. He understands that he should have found out what the going rate for advertising services was

3. He motivates himself by concentrating his energy on regaining his former position

4. He comes up with an effective plan of action to get out of his current predicament

Answer

Option 1: This option is incorrect. Simon may have been successful in his previous position, but he should try to reaffirm his abilities by reminding himself of what he's done right so far in his current goal.

Option 2: This option is correct. Simon recognizes that the root cause of the problem was the fact that he priced himself out of the market.

Option 3: This option is incorrect. Instead of trying to get back his previous job, Simon should capitalize on the experience and try to refocus on increasing the number of advertisers in his publication.

Option 4: This option is incorrect. Simon should focus on something he has greater control over and create a plan that will increase advertisers in his publication.

Case Study: Question 2 of 2

Rather than focusing on finding a new job, what could Simon have done to overcome this obstacle?

Options:

1. He might have applauded himself on the level of courage he needed to leave his former position

2. He could have lowered the rate he was charging for his advertising services

3. He should have come up with a more realistic goal for himself from the outset

4. He could have overlooked the low number of advertisers and continued with his plan of action

Answer

Option 1: This option is correct. By focusing on the strength needed to leave his previous position, Simon might have controlled his negative thoughts by realizing he was strong enough to overcome his current problem.

Option 2: This option is correct. Simon could have taken decisive action to attract new clients by trying to become more competitive.

Option 3: This option is incorrect. Simon's goal was achievable. To overcome his obstacle, he should have reaffirmed his abilities and learned from the lesson to continue with his goal.

Option 4: This option is incorrect. Simon needed to recognize what the cause of the problem was and come up with an alternative plan.

CHAPTER 3 - Bouncing Back with Perseverance and Resilience

CHAPTER 3 - Bouncing Back with Perseverance and Resilience

Section 1 - Qualities That Give You Bounce Back Ability

Section 2 - Turning Setbacks into Lessons Learned

Section 3 - Embracing Lessons Learned

Section 1 - Qualities That Give You Bounce Back Ability

Section 1 - Qualities That Give You Bounce Back Ability

Every organization needs people who can bounce back from setbacks. These people possess perseverance and resiliency.

It's possible to develop and nurture the qualities necessary to bounce back. These qualities are known as the 5 A's: absolute determination, ability to find meaning, adaptability and improvisation, action orientation, and acceptance of reality.

Absolute determination enables you to remain focused on your goals no matter what setbacks or struggles you face. Ability to find meaning will create a sense of purpose in your work. Adaptability and improvisation is the ability to look outside the obvious tools at hand to find a solution to problems.

Action orientation is based around self-awareness, self-management, accepting responsibility, and the ability to keep working. Acceptance of reality allows you to separate your own failures from setbacks outside of your control.

Dealing with setbacks

Dealing with setbacks

There's no exact science that enables someone to live a perfect life, nor is there a secret for a trouble-free career. In life and in business, there will be challenges, disruptions, and sometimes disappointments. This is why organizations need people who can bounce back from setbacks.

In an ever-evolving business environment, you have to be able to constantly adapt to survive. As organizations alter processes, procedures, and strategies, they still expect high levels of performance. This means each employee, manager, and executive must always keep pace with change.

You may have said that perseverance is essential for adapting to change. In any job area, perseverance enables you to achieve targets despite setbacks.

Resilience is another essential attribute for job-related success. Resiliency allows you to bounce back from adversity, and adapt to the changes surrounding you.

Lacking perseverance and resilience – and with them, the ability to bounce back – can be a major disadvantage. Consider the example of Evan, the finance manager for a sportswear firm. He's meeting with Greg, the research and development manager. Follow along as they discuss recent department productivity reports.

Evan: I can't believe how poor my department's productivity report is. We're down 30% from last year's figures, and I put every ounce of energy I had into trying to make us more productive.

Evan is upset.

Greg: I understand what you're saying but the only thing to do is bounce back and do better. My department got poor results last year because we were fatigued. We planned and organized our workflow better this year to combat that. I know my team has found this approach easier to work under and our productivity figures have almost doubled.

Greg is positive.

Evan: But that's your team - it's completely different for mine. Our current process is the only way to organize the workflow effectively. I guess there's nothing you can do when your team members just want to be home early every day.

Evan is angry.

Greg: Well it's our responsibility to motivate our teams and to get them to meet our departments' productivity targets. Last year, productivity was down 15% in my department so I used a more open approach with my team to work out a solution and we're getting good results.

Greg is concerned.

Evan: Really, I can't have this conversation right now. I need some space to think about things. I'll go back over all the productivity ratings. Then I'll see if the company got anything wrong. I just don't think the numbers reflect reality.

Evan is annoyed.

Greg: Evan, that's not the way to go. You're putting energy into what will really be a futile exercise. I know the executives who compile these productivity reports, and they have total faith in their methodology. They won't care about any faults you find, even if there are any.

Greg is sincere.

Evan: What do they want then?

Evan is upset.

Greg: They just want to show you how your team can improve. I think if you stepped back for a second and looked at this again, you'd see that.

Greg is serious.

The value of being able to bounce back is emphasized by Greg and Evan's conversation. Greg has had setbacks and bounced back, while Evan is struggling to follow suit. In Evan's case, he's suffering from burnout, and feeling he can't do anything more to help productivity. His attitude that his team's performance can't be any better shows a general pessimism regarding his situation. And believing that only Greg's team is capable of reversing poor productivity simply emphasizes Evan's cynicism.

During the conversation, Evan refuses to take any of Greg's sound advice. He doesn't think any advice can help

Perseverance and Resilience

his department bounce back, and this demonstrates a level of defensiveness.

Evan also falls into the trap of using an ineffective coping mechanism to ignore his problems. Instead of facing up to reality, he wants to spend energy proving the productivity figures wrong.

Question

What personality traits are common in people who find it difficult to bounce back from setbacks?

Options:

1. Having a general attitude of cynicism toward work and fellow employees

2. Feeling the need to talk to fellow employees about how best to recover from a setback

3. Relying on an unhealthy coping mechanism to get through a difficult time at work

4. Feeling the need to review errors in detail to find a solution to the setback

Answer

Option 1: This option is correct. A general attitude of cynicism toward work is common among those who find it difficult to bounce back. These people feel they can't do anything to solve the situation they face.

Option 2: This option is incorrect. Those who find it difficult to bounce back from setbacks will often avoid the issue altogether.

Option 3: This option is correct. Those finding it difficult to bounce back may concentrate their energy on coping mechanisms. This action is a way of avoiding the situation at hand.

Option 4: This option is incorrect. Those who find it difficult to bounce back from disappointment will try to avoid reviewing the reasons for it.

Being determined and finding meaning

Being determined and finding meaning

The qualities needed to bounce back can be developed and nurtured. These qualities are the 5 A's: absolute determination, ability to find meaning, adaptability and improvisation, action orientation, and acceptance of reality.

The first of the 5 A's, absolute determination, is the ability to stay focused on your goals. You have to be determined but also open minded to see your goals through from start to finish. By being open minded, you can adapt or be flexible in your approach to situations.

You must focus on just what it is you want to achieve. It could be a financial goal, a productivity target, or a change in company processes. Set a time frame to achieve this goal and focus your actions on completing it.

Always maintain your focus. This will help sustain you as you face obstacles or struggles.

Consider the example of Amber, who manages a gym that experienced a 15% slump in profits last year. Determined to reverse this trend, she reduces fees and purchases new equipment. Following these moves, Amber targets a 10% upturn in profits within six months. However, the company's profits remain static for the following three months. Amber takes a colleague's advice to also introduce new fitness classes. This move helps raise monthly profits, and Amber reaches her 10% target within six months.

Question

Stewart is a project manager for a confectionary company. He's aiming to introduce a new product to the company's offerings before the upcoming holiday season. However, following the results of a focus group's taste test, the company's directors decide the product isn't ready for market.

What examples of Stewart's behavior following this setback indicate that he possesses the quality of absolute determination?

Options:

1. Stewart moves away from his original idea and begins developing a new product

2. Stewart keeps his focus on getting the product ready in time for the upcoming holiday season

3. Stewart is open minded regarding the focus group's criticism and studies its comments

4. Stewart assembles a new focus group to see if it thinks the product is ready for market

Answer

Perseverance and Resilience

Option 1: This option is incorrect. Stewart has strayed from his original focus of getting the tested product to market.

Option 2: This option is correct. By keeping his focus, Stewart is demonstrating absolute determination. He has a goal set out and is continuing to focus on it.

Option 3: This option is correct. Being open minded allows a determined Stewart to see how he can best recover from his setback.

Option 4: This option is incorrect. Stewart needs to convince his company's directors about the product rather than another focus group.

The second of the 5 A's – the ability to find meaning – helps to give a sense of purpose to your task. When your goal has meaning for you, you're better equipped to handle any setbacks.

Organizations often build a value system around the meaning of employees' jobs. Using this system can help you focus on the meaning of your job during difficult times.

If your work gives you a sense of satisfaction, you're more likely to do it well. Job satisfaction revolves around your own expectations and attitude.

To help find meaning in your job, identify your satisfaction triggers. Pinpoint what makes your job satisfactory for you. Then focus on triggering this feeling as often as possible.

Consider the example of Jorge, who works as a designer with a games developer. He was passed over for a promotion, and he's feeling a little depressed. He examines a new project he's been assigned that is extremely important to the company. The project appeals to Jorge's design strengths and his enthusiasm for it helps him regain a sense of job satisfaction. He also realizes how important his creative and artistic input is to his organization's success.

Question

Match the examples of employee behavior with the qualities they reflect. Each quality may match to more than one example.

Options:

A. Emile asks coworkers if they have any ideas on how he can improve his sales figures

B. Phil settles on a strict time frame for achieving his productivity targets

C. Leon finds he attains job satisfaction when he gets to work on creative projects

D. Mario loses a contract and is feeling disappointed but in a performance review he's reassured his role is vital to the company

Targets:

1. Ability to find meaning
2. Absolute determination

Answer

Leon's recognition of what gives him job satisfaction is key in finding meaning to his job. Mario meanwhile, can find meaning in his job despite disappointment, as his company's performance review reminds him of his importance.

Emile asking his coworkers for advice on his productivity indicates he's open minded. This is an essential element of absolute determination, as is setting a time line for achieving goals, which Phil does.

Adaptability, action, and acceptance

Adaptability, action, and acceptance

Possessing absolute determination and being able to find meaning creates the groundwork for bouncing back. Dealing with disruptions and setbacks throughout your career requires more qualities, though. Your actions are as vital as your attitude when it comes to the ability to bounce back. That's why the third of the 5 A's, adaptability and improvisation, is crucial.

Adaptability and improvisation enables resilient people to find creative solutions to problems. This means you're inventive with the resources available. With creative thinking, you'll be open to new ideas and enthusiastic about exploring alternative methods.

Consider the example of Chelsea, who's the financial manager of a major film production company. In the past year, the company has grown rapidly due to the success of several productions. There's been a 200% increase in staff and the introduction of a special effects department. The company has also set up offices in several new countries to target international markets.

Chelsea's latest budget was rejected by the company's CEO for not taking these new circumstances into account. Chelsea's past budgets were based on the previous year's figures. However, the growth of the company means she has to examine each department's budget plan again.

She adapts to this new situation by changing how the budget is constructed. Each department must now report to her with preliminary budget submissions. Then the department managers must meet with her to justify their department budgets. Finally, Chelsea will approve department budgets and the master budget after consulting with the company's CEO.

Question

What actions reflect the ability to adapt and improvise?

Options:

1. Remaining enthusiastic and looking for new after-sales processes after the loss of a major customer

2. Maintaining belief that the answer to your problems lies in established procedures

3. Accepting that only certain elements of a setback were under your control

4. Assembling a brainstorming session with coworkers to discuss creative ideas to recover from poor financial results

Answer

Option 1: This option is correct. Looking for alternative methods with enthusiasm will help you and those around you bounce back.

Option 2: This option is incorrect. Once you're faced with a problem that can't be solved through established procedures, you must adapt and look outside them.

Option 3: This option is incorrect. While it's helpful to have this realization, it doesn't assist in adapting or improvising to solve the issue at hand.

Option 4: This option is correct. Creative thinking will help you adapt and improvise. Using a brainstorming session, or simply talking to other employees, can help this process.

The fourth of the 5 A's is action orientation. It's based around four core ideals. The first two are self-awareness and self-management. Third, you have to be ready to accept responsibility, and finally you must keep working.

Self-awareness

Being self-aware means knowing how you think, feel, and react to situations, including setbacks and challenges. People who are self-aware can identify reasons for their success or failure.

Self-management

It's not enough to simply be aware of your strengths and weakness. You also need to know what to do with this information. Self-management involves assessing yourself and working out what actions you need to take to succeed.

Accept responsibility

Bouncing back from failure always involves taking responsibility for your actions and reactions. You're not responsible for everything that happens around you. However, you are responsible for your reactions to events. If something that's under your control results in a setback, take responsibility for it.

Keep working

Those with the ability to bounce back will always keep working toward a solution. Even when faced with obstacles and setbacks, they keep taking action to overcome them.

The fifth of the 5 A's is acceptance of reality. You need to be aware of the reality of your situation, and separate fact from opinions and feelings. This allows you to understand when failures are within or outside of your control.

Imagine you're a web security sales manager who has just failed to win an important contract. However this only happened because the client decided it can't afford the technology. Your pitch for the contract may have been perfect, and the technology may suit the client. However, the client's final decision not to use the technology is out of your control.

Being realistic in your evaluation of a situation will stop you from blaming yourself needlessly. It allows you to distinguish between self-perceived failure and actual setbacks.

Being realistic in your evaluation involves avoiding unwarranted pessimism and false optimism. Unwarranted pessimism is a damaging emotion which convinces people that, no matter what happens, they're doomed to face failure. Bouncing back from a setback requires analysis rather than concluding that nothing can be changed.

Conversely, acceptance of reality is also hindered by false optimism. Equally as damaging as pessimism, it occurs when people are too optimistic about their ability to bounce back. Those who haven't faced adversity may think they're resilient but haven't actually proved it.

Perseverance and Resilience

Unfortunately, resilience is something that is only ever discovered after you've faced a setback.

Question

Match the examples of employee behavior with the qualities they represent.

Options:

A. Tim pinpoints a job satisfaction trigger and focuses on reaching this as often as possible

B. Justin realizes his accounting error didn't lead to a flawed company budget

C. Gary knows he can only edit product assessment reports if he's tested the product personally D. Sasha has set a time frame for completing her employee assessments

E. Theresa finds a new way of monitoring IT performance when previous methods fail

Targets:

1. Acceptance of reality
2. Action orientation
3. Adaptability and improvisation
4. Ability to find meaning
5. Absolute determination

Answer

As Justin realizes that his error isn't responsible for a bigger failure, he's accepting reality. He must know when to take the blame for a setback and when not to.

Gary's knowledge of when he can edit assessment reports is a result of self-awareness and self-management. These are core elements of action orientation.

Theresa's ability to find a new solution to monitoring IT performance shows an ability to adapt and improvise when faced with a setback.

Tim's discovery of a satisfaction trigger is an example of finding meaning. By reaching this target as much as possible, enjoyment of his job increases with it.

Sasha's decision to set a time frame for completing her assessments shows absolute determination. Doing this will help her focus on achieving her target.

Section 2 - Turning Setbacks into Lessons Learned

Section 2 - Turning Setbacks into Lessons Learned

Everyone will experience setbacks and failures at some point. However, it's important to realize these can be used as a learning experience. While it may be difficult to assess reasons for failure, it's vital you focus on the causes of it in order to fully recover. This process helps you to move on, adapt, and persevere.

When you experience a setback, you should always aim to learn a lesson from it. Achieving this usually involves four major steps. First, identify what went wrong by viewing the setback from varying perspectives. Second, identify why it went wrong and determine whether the causes were beyond your control or not.

Next, identify how you can avoid having it happen again. This means noting everything that went wrong, accepting fault if necessary, and reflecting on the lessons you can learn. Finally, create a lessons learned documents to see where you got things right and where you can improve.

Learning from failure

Have you ever read a novel or seen a movie where the people all lived happily ever after? Imagine if real life were like that. Imagine if all your endeavors inevitably led to success. However, in the real world, you'll meet with failure as well as success. You'll have to face setbacks and overcome obstacles. Even though you might not live happily ever after, you can learn how to cope with failure and bounce back to work toward your goals.

You might regard your failure as a negative experience. Although it's not always pleasant, failure can become a learning experience for you. Through a process of trial and error, you learn what works and what doesn't work. You may encounter many failures on your road to success.

Perseverance and Resilience

Significant failures must be seen as an opportunity for both external and internal learning. External learning is about what your actions project. If you experience a setback and react in a certain way – anger, calmness, or confusion – what does that say about you to others?

Internal learning relates to the person you are, as well as the type of employee or colleague you are. Look inwards to what internal qualities of yours contributed to the setback. Perhaps you're unable to accept help, prone to rushing matters, or are too quiet.

A key aspect of perseverance and resilience is your ability when faced with a setback to acknowledge that a lot can be learned from it. External and internal learning are key to this. Consider the example of event manager Lydia. She recently supplied the wrong date for a festival press release. Lydia initially blamed this error on her designer. However, she soon realized it was her own mistake, made because she was working on too many projects at once.

From this setback, Lydia realized that externally she may be seen as an individual who blames others after a setback. She will work on correcting this. Also, analyzing what caused the setback – her working on too many projects at once – gives her an opportunity for internal learning. She realizes she doesn't find it easy to ask for help when she needs it. She also notes that she finds it difficult to delegate responsibility.

Turning a setback into a lesson

Turning a setback into a lesson

Failure can be difficult to recover from because it often brings about strong emotions. However, you have to take a step back from the experience and try to identify why you failed. Then you can take steps to avoid making the same mistakes in the future. It takes perseverance to move beyond immediate emotions and review the reasons for failure.

When dissecting a setback, you must be objective. Look at the facts of the situation and avoid relying on emotions or opinions. Don't dwell on the mistake, endlessly asking yourself what you should've done. Instead, dissect the situation fully and see what you can learn from it. Having analyzed what went wrong, develop positive lessons from the experience. These show you how to best move forward and grow from a challenge.

Perseverance and Resilience

Popular in business lore is the story of the IBM executive who was summoned to CEO Tom Watson's office in the 1960s – shortly after making a decision that lost the company $10 million. The executive expected to be fired and was surprised when Watson replied, "Fire you? ... Of course not. I've just spent $10 million educating you."

This story highlights how you can receive a positive return on your failures and setbacks. Your mistakes may have come at a cost, but do not forget potential gains such as knowledge, innovation opportunities, and other unexpected benefits.

Think about gains from failures as a three step process. Firstly, identify what specifically went wrong. Next, look at why it went wrong by analyzing your failure. Finally, examine your failure gains. So you can ask yourself, what was the failure, why did the failure occur, and what gains can be taken from the failure?

Question

Which statement is true about gains from failures?

Options:

1. Making gains from failures means recognizing that any time and money invested in the failed endeavor is a sunk cost – moving forward quickly is the best option.

2. Making gains from failures means recognizing key take-aways from the experience that can lead to future successes: such as increased knowledge or a new innovation.

Answer

Option 1: This option is incorrect. You are leaving behind valuable currency if you choose not to take time to examine your failure and use it as a learning experience.

Option 2: This option is correct. Making gains from failures means reaming new knowledge that can lead you to success in future endeavors. You view your failure as a learning opportunity and are now using that experience to improve different aspects of your work.

Identifying causes of failure

Making gains from your failures is the basis for how you can turn a setback into a lesson learned. On a basic level, turning a setback into a lesson learned requires four steps. First, identify what went wrong. Second, identify why it went wrong. Third, identify how you can avoid it from happening again. Finally, create a lessons learned document.

The first step - identifying what went wrong - involves several tasks:
- collect all the evidence surrounding the setback,
- build a time line of events that led to the setback,
- create a problem statement, which pinpoints what the exact issue was that led to the setback, and
- determine the contributing factors that led to the situation.

Following a setback, causal analysis is perhaps the best way to collect evidence and build a time line. This involves viewing setbacks from varied perspectives, and placing many factors under consideration. Your thoughts regarding the reasons for a setback commonly affect your reaction. Overriding these thoughts with analysis helps you reach a more reasoned conclusion.

For example, Colin works as an interior designer and his latest project was a month late. He's at a loss to explain exactly what happened so he performs a causal analysis. Colin researches the meetings connected with the project and the hours he worked on it. He then builds a time line of what happened, discovering that he spent too much time meeting with the client. He creates a problem statement, which pinpoints this as the cause for the delay.

Question

Rose manages the engineering team at a television manufacturer and her team has suffered a setback. The team's design for a touchscreen remote control was deemed too expensive to manufacture.

Following this setback, what actions will help Rose when trying to identify what went wrong?

Options:

1. She should collect the evidence surrounding the design process of the remote control

2. She should begin the process of a second design for the remote control

3. She should go about creating a problem statement on the setback

4. She should take aside a single colleague to ask for thoughts on what went wrong

Perseverance and Resilience

5. She should try to construct a time line of the events which led to setback

6. She should determine what exactly were the contributing factors that led to the setback

Answer

Option 1: This option is correct. By collecting the evidence of what happened during the design process, Rose can determine which element, or elements, led to the project's failure.

Option 2: This option is incorrect. Beginning a second design leaves no time to identify what went wrong the first time.

Option 3: This option is correct. Once Rose finds out what went wrong, she should create a problem statement confirming the root cause. This will help her avoid similar mistakes again.

Option 4: This option is incorrect. Asking one colleague alone will only gain limited knowledge when trying to collect all the evidence.

Option 5: This option is correct. After Rose collects evidence of what happened, she should piece it together in a time line.

Option 6: This option is correct. By determining the contributing factors that led to the touchscreen setback, Rose can recognize them if they occur again in the future.

Following a setback, after identifying what went wrong, the second step is to identify why it went wrong. Central to this is determining whether the causes of the setback were beyond your control or not.

This means going one step further to determine the root cause. For example, remember Colin the interior designer? He discovered that the reason for a delayed project was too much time being devoted to meeting his client.

Next, he analyzed why he spent so much time meeting with the client. Reading between the lines, he came to the conclusion that he had given signs to his client that he could be involved in all the details of the project. As this client is very detail-oriented, he was called to several meetings regarding minor decisions.

Question

Was the root cause of Colin's setback beyond his control?

Options:

1. Yes
2. No

Answer

Option 1: This option is incorrect. Colin's behavior had an impact on the root cause of the setback. By being clearer and limiting his involvement, he could have avoided meeting with the client so often.

Option 2: This option is correct. Had Colin made it clear to his client that he shouldn't be consulted over minor details, there would not have been the damaging volume of meetings.

Avoiding setbacks in the future

Avoiding setbacks in the future

In the aftermath of a failure, you need to identify what exactly happened and why. In order to turn a setback into a lesson learned, you have to carry out the third step in the process and avoid making the same mistake again. Repeating the mistake would represent an even bigger failure.

To avoid repeating errors, be analytical. In the face of a failure, make a list of your actions and figure out which actions were ultimately wrong. This list can act as a reminder of possible errors when working on similar projects.

To move on, always admit your mistakes. If you've made an error, don't be too proud to admit it. Without acknowledging what you've done wrong, it's difficult to learn lessons from the experience.

You need to take corrective actions to prevent similar errors in the future. Look at the root causes of a setback. What changes can stop such setbacks from happening again?

Corrective actions will help to ensure you don't make the same mistakes again. Admittedly, the situation surrounding a failure will usually be a one time thing. However, though each setback may be unique, you can glean universal lessons from the situation. These lessons learned can then be used in all manner of situations in the future.

Consider the example of a photographer, Sinead, who's analyzing a recent setback. She failed to win a contract as a national newspaper's sports photographer. Sinead has come to the conclusion that the setback was due to an unprofessional pitch for the contract.

A month later, Sinead is competing for a lucrative contract with an events organizer. Sinead wants to use the lessons learned from the newspaper setback. After researching what other people have done in similar situations, she changes the approach of her pitch. She also talks to a recruitment consultant about changing her overall performance in such meetings. This leads to her focusing on the technical details of her photography and her portfolio when meeting with the events organizer.

Dissecting a setback can be a difficult task. To keep track of the revelations that arise during this process, create a lessons learned document. This is the fourth step in turning a setback into a valuable learning process. The lessons learned document is split into three sections: areas that were successful, areas that need improvement, and general lessons learned information.

Perseverance and Resilience

Areas that were successful

A setback may be due to one element among many going wrong. Along with the offending error there may have been several successes.

Consider the example of a motorcycle engine manufacturer that fails to meet a production target due to insufficient materials. The production manager may be responsible, but there may also have been accompanying successes to note. For instance, a new production methodology may have been successfully tested.

Areas that need improvement

During the dissection of your setback, you'll notice areas that can be improved upon.

For example, an online retailer's budgeting process falters due to the accountant's lack of delegation skills. This leads to the budget being rushed and not having sufficient detail. Both the company and the accountant can document this area as requiring improvement.

General lessons learned information

As you document the reasons for a setback, certain categories will stand out.

For example, if a toy company fails to reach a financial target, obvious elements of the business are dissected. These include sales and marketing, with both providing lessons to learn from. However, beyond these sections of the business, the company can also find general lessons learned information in areas such as product design or even working conditions.

Question

Match the actions with the relevant steps in turning a setback into a lesson learned. Each step may apply to more than one action.

Options:
A. Ted admitted that he didn't pay enough attention to preparing notes for a failed business meeting
B. After a poor performance review, Josh noted areas of his approach to work that can be improved upon
C. Despite his architectural design not meeting a client's approval, Clive noted that many elements of the design were approved
D. Jenny made a list of all the actions involved in creating her failed mission statement

Targets:
1. Identify how you can avoid it from happening again
2. Create a lessons learned document

Answer

By admitting his mistake, Ted has identified where his business meeting went wrong. This highlights a mistake he will want to avoid happening again. Likewise, Jenny's list of actions highlighted where she went wrong, and what actions she should avoid in future.

Josh's decision to note areas of where his approach to work can be improved will make up a vital part of a lessons learned document. And in the document, Clive can learn through noting the areas he was successful in an ultimately failed project.

Case Study: Question 1 of 3
Scenario

Richard is the marketing manager for a soft drinks company. Recently he managed the launch of a new orange-flavored drink. Though the product had the same amount of calories as the company's regular soft drinks, Richard decided to market it in a similar fashion to a health-conscious product.

Perseverance and Resilience

The marketing strategy caused great confusion with customers and retailers. Eventually there was so much bad publicity surrounding the drink that the product was recalled.

Answer the questions on how Richard can turn this setback into a lesson learned, in order.

Question

Richard begins with causal analysis of the situation which led to the product recall.

What does this process entail?

Options:

1. Richard builds a time line of the events which led to the decision to market the drink as a health-conscious product

2. Richard tells colleagues that it was his fault the drink was marketed as being a health-conscious product

3. Richard makes notes on the successful elements in the marketing campaign

4. Richard determines whether or not the failure of the marketing campaign was beyond his control

Answer

Option 1: This option is correct. During causal analysis, it's important for Richard to draw up this time line. It will help indicate what contributed to the setback.

Option 2: This option is incorrect. While this is a good idea, this won't happen at the stage of causal analysis. Instead, once causal analysis is finished, Richard can properly decipher whether the setback was his fault of not.

Option 3: This option is incorrect. Noting the successful elements of the campaign is useful but it's done at a later stage.

Option 4: This option is correct. At the stage of causal analysis, Richard will be able to determine if the campaign's failure was within his control. Whether it was his fault will require further investigation though.

Case Study: Question 2 of 3

Richard lists the actions that led to the new soft drink being recalled.

What else should he do at this point to help turn this setback into a lesson learned?

Options:

1. Richard should analyze why his campaign portrayed the drink as a healthy alternative

2. Richard should create an alternative marketing campaign using the lessons learned from the setback

3. Richard should admit to senior executives it was his mistakes in the marketing campaign that led to the product recall

4. Richard should take on board the lesson that marketing campaigns must be based on fact

Answer

Option 1: This option is incorrect. This process should take place earlier, as a result of causal analysis.

Option 2: This option is incorrect. Richard hasn't fully learned the lessons from this setback. He should wait until he's drawn up a lessons learned document to do this.

Option 3: This option is correct. By admitting his errors, Richard can concentrate on making sure they don't happen again.

Option 4: This option is correct. Once Richard realizes the mistakes that led to the failed product launch, he should learn from them.

Case Study: Question 3 of 3

If Richard decides to draw up a lessons learned document, what should he include in it?

Options:

1. Richard should draw up guidelines on consulting marketing experts in the early stages of any other major campaigns

2. Richard should list what went wrong in the early stages in the soft drink's marketing campaign

3. Richard should devote a section to how the company has recovered from similar setbacks before

4. Richard should take note of the successful elements to the campaign such as how the product packaging was aesthetically pleasing

5. Richard should note how he's learned that in future he must be truthful with customers over the contents of a product

Answer

Option 1: This option is correct. This can be part of a section that addresses the work practices that can be improved upon following the setback.

Option 2: This option is incorrect. This type of list doesn't belong in a lessons learned document, but would be of use during causal analysis.

Option 3: This option is incorrect. The lessons learned document should concentrate on the setback in question rather than previous ones.

Option 4: This option is correct. Richard should remember the elements of his marketing strategy which were successful, instead of completely changing how he works.

Option 5: This option is correct. Richard details any lessons he's learned in the document.

Section 3 - Embracing Lessons Learned
Section 3 - Embracing Lessons Learned

Even the most successful people you know will experience setbacks at some point. When faced with failure though, the important thing is not to let it define you. Don't dwell on a setback, instead embrace the lessons learned from it.

There are four strategies to embracing setbacks as lessons learned. The first strategy is to control the message. Take the positive points from the experience and emphasize them both to yourself and those around you. The second strategy is to re-evaluate your goals. Reassess both the short-term and long-

term targets that may have contributed to your setback. Revise your goals as necessary so that you don't repeat the same mistakes.

The third strategy is to reflect on what you'll do differently in the future. This process asks you to stop looking back at a failure and instead take lessons from it to shape future decisions. Finally, establish a regained sense of confidence, one that's boosted by the knowledge you've gained from the experience of a setback.

Don't let failure define you

Don't let failure define you

Perseverance and resiliency will help you turn a setback into lessons learned. Any failure should be looked upon as an opportunity to improve. For some people that's not an easy task and some may let a setback or failure define them.

Consider the example of Lynsey, who works in the Finance Department of a cosmetics firm. One of her responsibilities is to purchase materials for the company's products. She recently went on vacation, leaving instructions for a colleague to do this. However, the instructions she left had incorrect details, resulting in insufficient materials purchased for production. This halted production on several products. Follow along as Lynsey talks to the company's accountant, Ian, about how the situation has affected her.

Lynsey: I still can't believe I got those figures wrong while I was away. I can barely face coming into work since I came back.
Lynsey is stressed.
Ian: It can't be that bad. I mean that was two weeks ago. Trust me, everyone's forgotten about it.
Ian is positive.
Lynsey: No, they haven't! I can feel that no one has any confidence in my work now. I'm double-checking everything I do now, triple-checking even. I'm actually falling behind in my workload because of it too.
Lynsey is worried.
Ian: Seriously, it's one error, the only one I can remember you ever making. You were warned about it at the time and it's done. Move on and learn from it.
Ian is concerned.
Lynsey: I'd like to, but I know no one is going to trust my work anymore. If I don't, why would anyone else?
Lynsey is stressed.
Ian: You've really got to get past this. Everyone makes mistakes. Seriously, it wasn't that bad.
Ian is concerned.
Lynsey: I wish I could believe that but I know what I'd think about someone else who made this mistake. I'd say they're not up to the job.
Lynsey is downhearted.

Lynsey has made the error of letting her mistake define her. She now thinks of herself as a failure. She concentrates on the mistake and lets it define how she approaches work each day. Lynsey is now being overly careful with her work and falling behind as a result. This course of events may lead to more mistakes in the future as her workload builds. She will only get back on track if she can move past this setback.

Question

When you experience a setback, how does it affect you?

Options:

1. I let it define me
2. I try to move on by not thinking about it anymore
3. I learn from it and embrace the lessons learned

Answer

Option 1: You say you let a setback define you. This is a common occurrence following a setback, however it's also damaging. You have to move past a particular failure, learn from it, and use the experience gained from it.

Option 2: You choose to move on by not thinking about the setback anymore. This is a common approach for many people following a setback. However, by not examining the setback, you can't learn valuable lessons from it.

Option 3: You say you learn from your lessons and embrace them. This is a healthy way of looking at a setback. When you dissect the error, failure, or mistake there are lessons to learn from it. You then have to embrace these lessons and move on positively following your setback.

To help you embrace the lessons learned from a setback, you can use four strategies. First, control the message about the setback. Then re-evaluate your goals and reflect on what you'll do differently in future. Finally, establish a regained sense of confidence.

The first strategy to embracing lessons learned from a setback is to control the message. This means viewing the setback in a positive light, something which begins with you. You have to communicate encouraging messages to yourself regarding the failure you've experienced.

Find the positives in your setback. Just as you allow yourself to feel pride after a success, tell yourself that you can find plusses in your failure. Consider the example of a web designer who creates a site for a prospective client. The client rejects the design, but the designer believes it can be used to upgrade the web sites of existing clients.

Use positive mental images of what can be achieved following a failure. By managing to keep your mind in a positive state, you can begin to manage the situation. For instance, Jack, the owner of a theatre production company suffers a setback when a new play fails financially. Jack thinks about companies in similar circumstances that have gone on to produce successful plays. These images help him remain positive and he urges his employees to have a similar outlook.

The words "failure," "error," or "setback" carry negative connotations. When examining a failure, error, or setback of your own, don't think of it in these terms. Move on from these words and refer to the experience as a learning opportunity instead.

When talking about a setback, you need to manage the story and the interpretation of it. Take an audio equipment salesperson who fails to reach an agreement with a major client. To avoid overreaction from those around him, the salesperson assures fellow employees he understands why this happened. He also tries to find a solution to it.

Be calm and view a setback as something that provides valuable information for the future. Communicate this idea to those around you. Once they view the setback in this manner, you've successfully controlled the message about it.

For example, Trevor is a clothing retailer's social media specialist. He recently managed a campaign to attract new customers but research showed it appealed only to existing customers. The campaign was seen as wasteful by colleagues. Trevor remains positive, however, as he realizes lessons can be learned from the situation. He refuses to refer to the setback as a "failure." He tells colleagues it actually showed them what to do when targeting existing customers. His colleagues soon see the campaign in this light as well.

Question

How can you help to control the message about a setback you've experienced?

Options:

1. Don't listen to what others are saying and concentrate on moving on

2. Manage any stories regarding the setback within your company

3. State that you have a solution to the setback in question, then examine it fully

4. When thinking about the setback, communicate positive messages to yourself regarding it

Answer

Option 1: This option is incorrect. It's best to face up to a setback and try to manage how you and others view it.

Option 2: This option is correct. By managing how people within the company perceive the setback, you can help to ultimately turn it into a positive. Don't overreact to a setback. Instead, calmly assure others that lessons can be learned from it.

Option 3: This option is incorrect. It's unwise to state that you can repair a setback before you've examined it fully. Only when you have all the details can you see whether you can solve it.

Option 4: This option is correct. Having a positive mindset in the wake of a setback is crucial. Tell yourself that positives can be gained from this process.

By dissecting a setback, you can uncover the lessons that can be learned from it. Use these lessons to ask yourself if it's necessary to re-evaluate your goals. This is the second strategy for helping you embrace the lessons learned from a setback. It enables you to ask if your original goals were too optimistic or if particular short-term goals could have helped you avoid your setback. Revise your goals as necessary so that you don't repeat the same mistakes.

Reassess where you've been - think about the lessons learned from previous setbacks, and how they've helped you. Also, reassess where you are. Think about how your current attitude toward work has been affected by knowledge gained from setbacks. Then, reassess where you're going. Think about how your future will be shaped with all the knowledge you now possess. Re-evaluate your goals by finding new areas in which you can succeed in the future.

Consider the example of Adele, a saleswoman with a data center specialist. At the beginning of each year, she sets out short-term targets for quarterly sales, and a long-term target for annual sales. Last year she experienced a setback when her manager said her targets lacked ambition. She doesn't want to repeat this error so she sets

Perseverance and Resilience

large sales targets. However, in the first quarter of the year, she fails to reach her intended figures.

Adele soon realizes she set an unrealistic target for herself for the first quarter. She looks upon this current failure as an opportunity to learn. As she reassesses where she's been, she notes how last year's setback taught her she wasn't ambitious enough. She feels it was this realization that affected her overly ambitious sales targets this time.

Adele begins to think about where she's going, and re-evaluates her goals in terms of the next quarter's sales targets. In addition, Adele re-evaluates her sales goals for the other two quarters this year, and her long-term annual sales target. Like Adele, re-evaluating your short-term goals may require changes to your long-term goals too.

Question

Match the action to the appropriate strategy for embracing lessons learned. Each strategy may have more than one match.

Options:

A. Una reassesses her monthly sales target after failing to reach last month's figures

B. Dean tells his employees they should see a recent sales setback as an opportunity to learn

C. The lessons Carol learns from a business setback encourage her to change product direction for her company

D. Leo tells himself that a failed product design has taught him valuable lessons

Targets:

1. Control the message about the setback
2. Re-evaluate your goals

Answer

Sorin Dumitrascu

Dean telling his employees to view a setback as an opportunity and Leo learning lessons from a failed design are examples of controlling the message. It's essential to control the message a setback sends to others, but also to have a positive mindset in the face of failure too.

Una's decision to reassess her monthly goals and Carol's new direction following a setback are typical of people re-evaluating their goals. Many who experience a setback benefit from reassessing short-term goals and finding new areas in which they can succeed through lessons learned.

Moving forward after failure

Moving forward after failure

Having analyzed a setback, you should have a good idea of why it happened. The next step is to reflect on what you'll do differently in the future. This process is the third strategy for embracing the lessons learned from a setback. It asks you to stop thinking in terms of "what if," and start thinking in terms of "next time I will."

Reflecting on what you'll do differently from now on means changes to your work practices. This doesn't necessarily mean more hours in the office. Rather it's about thinking strategically. Perhaps you need to cut down the number of meetings you attend, or increase the amount of work you delegate to others. In short, what can you change to avoid setbacks in the future?

Amy works in the Distribution Department of a watch manufacturer. Last month she made the error of mixing up several orders, with products going to the wrong addresses. Follow along as she talks to her colleague Chris about what she'll do differently in the future.

Amy: Hey Chris, how are you? I'm just finalizing the orders for this month.

Amy is positive.

Chris: I'm great....Are you nervous after last month? It's OK if you're stressed. It can happen.

Chris is concerned.

Amy: I'm actually okay. I've looked into where I went wrong and I know I can make sure it doesn't happen again. I made the mistake because I used estimates of orders from our sales team as the final order sheet.

Amy is happy.

Chris: So what's happening this time? Are you putting in more hours to double-check each order with each customer?

Chris is interested.

Amy: I am double-checking with customers to make sure orders are correct, but it's not taking up more time. Instead of asking the sales team for updated numbers each week, I've requested they only talk to me when they've confirmed orders. Chasing them used to take up a lot of my time. But I can use that time now to double-check confirmed orders.

Amy is very positive.

Amy has used the setback to not only change how she works but also to change how the sales team interacts with her. Reflecting on what she'll do differently following the setback has benefited her thanks to her strategic decision regarding order confirmations.

Chris was concerned Amy might be stressed after last month's mistake. It's common that following a failure people are stressed about moving on. New challenges will arise that carry with them risks of failure, and this prospect can induce stress. This can have a corrosive effect on any individual, giving rise to a feeling of helplessness.

It's important to focus on progress. When facing a challenge, don't fear the consequences of failure. Instead focus on how it can help you move onwards positively.

Question

Which of these actions indicate someone who's reflected on what they'll do differently in the wake of a setback?

Options:

1. Robert will see if his inventory procedures fail again this month before changing them

2. Despite a recent failure, Barry decides not to fear making a mistake on his upcoming project

3. Having managed a failed project recently, Joanne decides not to take on any similar projects

4. Dermot changes his invoicing procedures to avoid a repeat of a costly recent mix up

Answer

Option 1: This option is incorrect. If the procedures Robert uses have failed, he should think about altering them rather than waiting to see if they will happen again.

Option 2: This option is correct. Barry should concentrate on making progress after a setback, using the lessons he's learned from it, rather than fearing another failure.

Option 3: This option is incorrect. Joanne should use the lessons learned from the project failure to help on the new project.

Option 4: This option is correct. By improving his invoicing procedures, Dermot is using the experience of the recent mix up positively.

It's important to plan the changes you'll make after a setback. However, it's important to have the confidence to actually follow through on these plans. Establishing a regained sense of confidence is the fourth strategy for embracing your lessons learned.

Finding confidence can be a struggle for many people following a setback. It's common to lose your confidence after experiencing failure. However, it's important to understand that learning lessons from setbacks actually make you more experienced.

With this experience comes confidence that you can overcome similar situations you encounter. Having conquered and learned from one setback for instance, you're more likely to believe this will be the case in future.

You can boost your confidence by reinforcing your competence. Set short-term goals, achieve them, and then enjoy this achievement. Little by little, these achievements help build the confidence to persevere when faced with a setback.

Consider the example of Tina, who designs a monthly magazine. In the latest edition, she made an error by failing to include page numbers. Tina's confidence in her work has suffered due to this. She's also upset she won't get the chance to make up for the mistake for another month. To regain confidence, she sets small targets. As each of her article designs is approved, she allows herself time to celebrate this. With each successful design, her confidence increases.

Question

Perseverance and Resilience

Match the action to the appropriate strategy for embracing lessons learned. Each strategy may have more than one match.

Options:

A. Suzanne is opening a new restaurant and feels the failure of a previous one has given her vital experience

B. Paul focuses on succeeding in a new project despite it resembling a recent failure

C. Yvonne modifies her approach to team management in the wake of a recent failure

D. Keith recovers from a large manufacturing setback by setting himself achievable short-term goals

Targets:

1. Establish a regained sense of confidence
2. Reflect on what you'll do differently in future

Answer

Suzanne viewing a previous failure as giving her experience, and Keith setting achievable short-terms goals are examples of how to establish a regained sense of confidence. It's better to see a setback as ultimately benefiting you, and moving on from it with new successes.

Paul's focus on succeeding and Yvonne's modified approach to team management are examples of people who've reflected on what they'll do differently in the future. Not fearing a new challenge and Question

Match the action to the appropriate strategy for embracing lessons learned. Each strategy may have more than one match.

Options:

A. Suzanne is opening a new restaurant and feels the failure of a previous one has given her vital experience

B. Paul focuses on succeeding in a new project despite it resembling a recent failure

C. Yvonne modifies her approach to team management in the wake of a recent failure

D. Keith recovers from a large manufacturing setback by setting himself achievable short-term goals

Targets:

1. Establish a regained sense of confidence
2. Reflect on what you'll do differently in future

Answer

Suzanne viewing a previous failure as giving her experience, and Keith setting achievable short-terms goals are examples of how to establish a regained sense of confidence. It's better to see a setback as ultimately benefiting you, and moving on from it with new successes.

Paul's focus on succeeding and Yvonne's modified approach to team management are examples of people who've reflected on what they'll do differently in the future. Not fearing a new challenge and

Question

Match the action to the appropriate strategy for embracing lessons learned. Each strategy may have more than one match.

Options:

A. Suzanne is opening a new restaurant and feels the failure of a previous one has given her vital experience

B. Paul focuses on succeeding in a new project despite it resembling a recent failure

C. Yvonne modifies her approach to team management in the wake of a recent failure

D. Keith recovers from a large manufacturing setback by setting himself achievable short-term goals

Perseverance and Resilience

Targets:
1. Establish a regained sense of confidence
2. Reflect on what you'll do differently in future

Answer

Suzanne viewing a previous failure as giving her experience, and Keith setting achievable short-terms goals are examples of how to establish a regained sense of confidence. It's better to see a setback as ultimately benefiting you, and moving on from it with new successes.

Paul's focus on succeeding and Yvonne's modified approach to team management are examples of people who've reflected on what they'll do differently in the future. Not fearing a new challenge and admitting that changes have to be made are big steps forward.

Question

Karim is the founder of a small marketing agency who recently experienced a setback. He was responsible for failing to include a client's web site address in a mass leaflet campaign. The client has since parted ways with Karim's company. Following this setback, Karim realized he was taking on too much work himself. He's decided that he will now delegate responsibility for such leaflets to a trusted freelance editor.

What actions can help Karim to embrace the lessons learned from this setback?

Options:
1. Karim should keep track of similar mistakes by rival companies in their leaflets
2. Karim should tell new clients that the leaflet mistake doesn't matter in the long run
3. Karim should set a short-term goal of producing a error-free leaflet in his next client campaign

4. Karim should concentrate on how the leaflet failure highlighted how the company needed to be reorganized

5. Karim should document how he will now delegate 80% of the editing process to the freelance sub-editor

6. Karim should reassess future projects that are already agreed on to see how he can change his approach to them

Answer

Option 1: This option is incorrect. Karim should be embracing the lessons learned from his setback. By ignoring them and concentrating on the errors of others, he won't move forward.

Option 2: This option is incorrect. Karim needs to control the message regarding his setback, but this is the wrong way to do it. He should instead admit the mistake but emphasize how it's reinvigorated his determination to give high-quality service to all clients.

Option 3: This option is correct. By setting himself a short-term goal, Karim can regain confidence and begin to embrace the lessons he's learned from his setback.

Option 4: This option is correct. In realizing that the company needs to be reorganized, Karim is concentrating on the positive effect his error has had. He's controlling the message about the setback whenever he thinks about it.

Option 5: This option is correct. By documenting how he will change his editing procedures, Karim is reflecting on what he'll do differently from now on as he embraces the lessons from the setback.

Option 6: This option is correct. By reassessing what lies ahead, Karim is re-evaluating his goals. Future projects may have been agreed upon under previous work practices. He should look again to see what effect the new procedures will have on them.

REFERENCES

References
- **Crunch Point: The 21 Secrets to Succeeding When it Matters Most** - 2007, Brian Tracy, AMACOM
- **The Resiliency Advantage: Master Change, Thrive Under Pressure, and Bounce Back From** Setbacks - 2005, Al Siebert, Berrett-Koehler Publishers
- **Personal Development All-In-One for Dummies** - 2007, Rhena Branch et al., John Wiley & Sons
- **The Stress Effect: Why Smart Leaders Make Dumb Decisions – And What to do About it** - 2010, Henry L. Thompson, Jossey-Bass
- **Talent is Never Enough: Discover the Choices that Will Take You Beyond Your Talent** - 2007, John C. Maxwell, Thomas Nelson

- **Talent is Never Enough: Discover the Choices that Will Take You Beyond Your Talent** - 2007, John C. Maxwell, Thomas Nelson
- **Goal Setting: How to Create an Action Plan and Achieve Your Goals, Second Edition** - 2008, Susan B. Wilson and Michael S. Dobson, AMACOM
- **Big Things Happen When You Do the Little Things Right: A 5-Step Program to Turn Your Dreams into Reality** -1998, Don Gabor, Conversation Arts Media
- **Cross-Functional Teams: Working with Allies, Enemies, and Other Strangers** - 2003, Glenn M. Parker, Jossey-Bass
- **Harvard Business Review on Building Personal and Organizational Resilience** - 2003, Harvard Business School Publishing, Harvard Business Press

www.ingramcontent.com/pod-product-compliance
Lightning Source LLC
Chambersburg PA
CBHW020914180526
45163CB00007B/2728